Meet the neighbours

The Pickwicks live on the outskirts of a large town. They are friendly with the people next door and with a number of other families around about where they live.

Here are some of them.

The Coopers

The Blooms

The Newells

The Bhogals

The Kirkpatricks

Th...

These people who all live quite near to each other are called neighbours. The area they live in is called a **neighbourhood.**

Look carefully at the drawings.
Describe what each family is doing.
How many children are there altogether in these seven families?
What is the average number of children in each family?

How does this compare to the average for
*   your class?*
*   your neighbourhood?*
*   your own family?*

What is the average size of "the family" in the Pickwick's neighbourhood if these seven are fairly typical?
How does this compare to the average family size for your neighbourhood? your class?

1

Land-use areas

Key

Houses and gardens

Shops

School, church and grounds

Building site

Factories

Farm and fields

Woods

Park

Roads

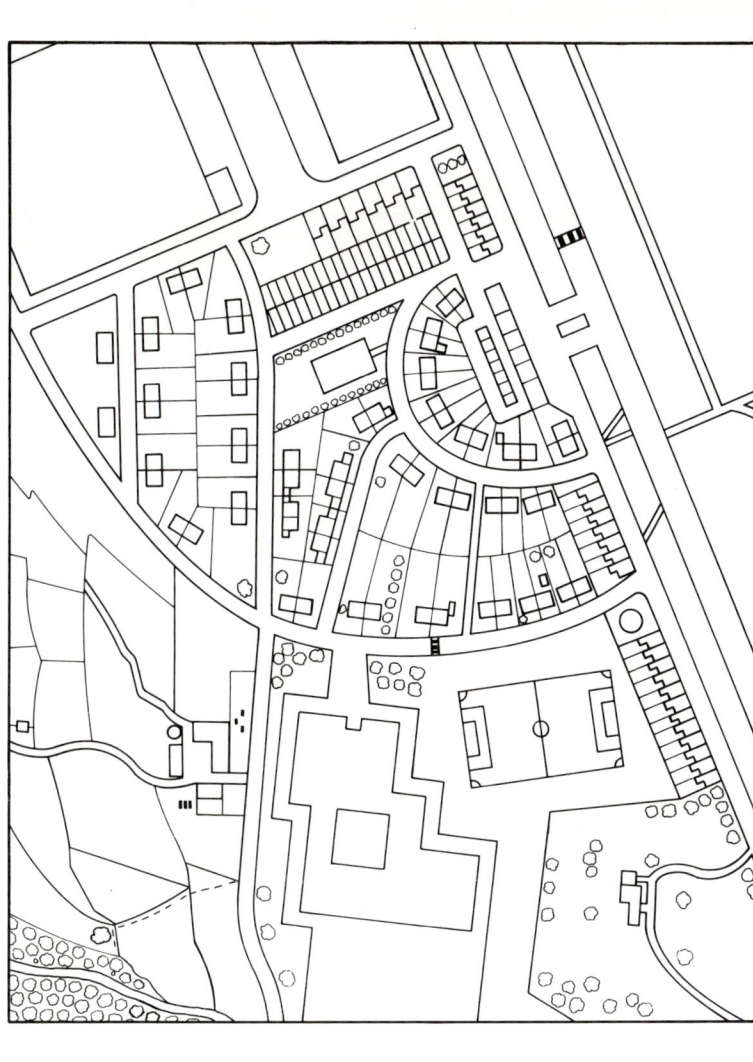

The neighbourhood

The picture above shows the neighbourhood where the Pickwicks and their friends live. The letters show where each family lives

(P = Pickwicks;   N = Newells;
C = Coopers;   B = Bhogals;
Bl = Blooms;   K = Kirkpatricks;   F = Fords).

As you can see, the land in this area is used in many different ways—for houses, for factories, for roads and so on.

Trace the sketch into your book and shade-in the different **land-use areas** *according to the key.*

In the right place add these words to your sketch: valley, main road.

Draw on your sketch the quickest route to follow when:
Richard Pickwick visits his friend Tersame Bhogal;
the Pickwicks go to the park;
Mrs Newell visits her friend who lives at the farm;
Mr Cooper goes to work at factory X.

Choose the words which best describe the patterns made by:
the houses and shops facing the main road;
the houses behind the shops;
the houses in front of the building site.

Words to choose from:
straight, linear, rectangular,
even, curved, crescent.

Houses in the neighbourhood—semis

Most people in the neighbourhood live in **semis**, i.e. semi-detached houses.

Turn to page 2 and list the five families who live in semis.

This picture shows a pair of modern semi-detached houses.

What are the walls made of?
What is the roof made of?
What other materials can you see *which are used in making a house?*
Do you know where we get these materials from?

Like most semis, these two were identical when they were built.

Write out these sentences using the right words from the brackets to fill the gaps:
  "Semi-detached houses share _____ wall(s)."
  (One; two; three.)
  "Semi-detached houses _____ a mirror image of each other.
  (Are; are not.)
  "A pair of semis _____ a good example of symmetry.
  (Is; is not.)

Although they were the same when built these two houses are already looking a little different.

Find three ways in which the people living here have tried to make them look different. Why do people do this?

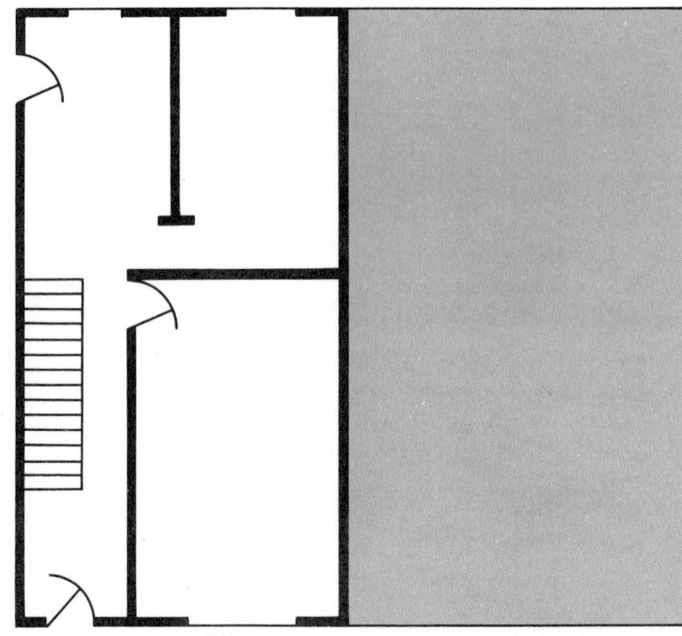

Here is the ground floor plan of one of the semis.

Copy the whole plan into your book and draw the ground floor plan of the other house.

This picture shows some older semi-detached houses.

How are they different from the new ones in the picture on page 4? (Think about such things as size, windows, roofs, gardens.) How are they the same as the houses in the picture on page 4?

One main difference is the way the older houses have their gardens enclosed.

List the different ways gardens have been marked off from the footpath and from the garden next door.
Why do houses and gardens have these boundaries?
Think of different reasons.
In the picture on page 4 find out what "H" stands for.
Streets often have signposts, pillar boxes, lampposts and other similar things. We call these the street **furniture**.
Describe the street furniture you can see in the picture on this page.

I WONDER WHAT THEY MEANT BY STREET FURNITURE. ~ I DON'T SEE ANY SEATS ABOUT!

Here is a piece of map showing an area of land 100 metres square (1 hectare).

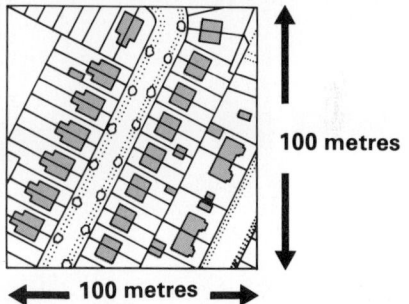

100 metres

100 metres

It is detailed enough to show each house, garden and garage. Pavements, verges and even trees are shown. All the houses are semi-detached.
Count the number of houses in this area and complete this sentence:
   In this area of 10,000 square metres there are _____ houses.

If an average of four people live in each house, how many people live in this area altogether? Do you think each house will have four people living in it? Why?

Here is a street of semi-detached houses. The figures show the number of people living in each house.

Copy and complete this sentence:
In this street of 100 metres there are _____ houses in which _____ people live.

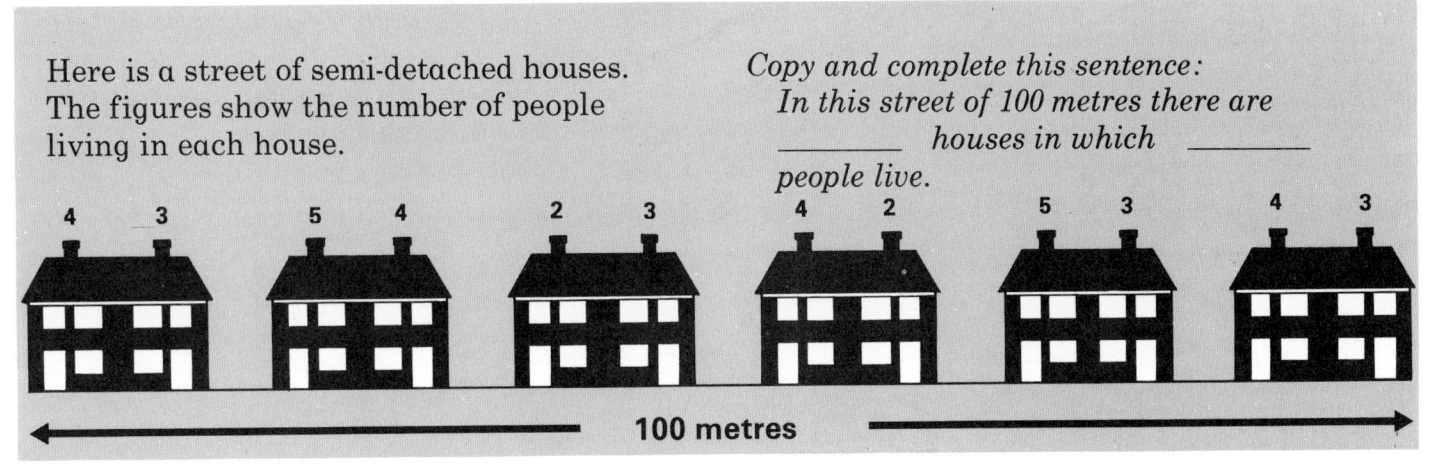

100 metres

Houses in the neighbourhood—terraces

Turn back to page 2 and find where the Coopers live.

Yes, they live in a **terrace** house.

Write about the position of the whole row of these houses—where it is from the main road, the school and the shops.
Where in the row is the Coopers' house?

This picture shows a terrace house.

Compare it with one of the semis on page 4.
Is this one older or younger?
Is this one wider or narrower? (You can measure the width of houses by counting bricks—a brick is 22½cm long.)
Is this one taller?
How many floors has each house?
Has this one more or less garden?
Have different building materials been used?
How many walls does this one share with other houses?

When these houses were built the builder went to some trouble to add decoration to make them look attractive.

Find and draw three different pieces of decoration.
Do you think the builder was successful in making these houses look attractive?

This picture shows the whole row of terrace houses.

The first nine were identical when built.

Write a few sentences describing what these houses look like. Remember to say how they are similar and how they are different.

Here is the ground floor plan of one of these terrace houses.

Copy the whole plan into your book and draw the ground floor plan of the house next door.

Are these houses mirror images of each other?

Draw the ground floor plan of your own house.

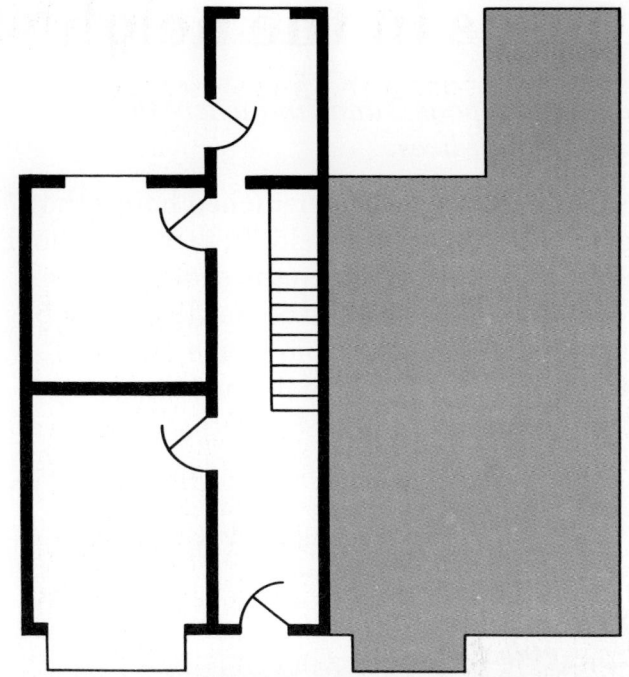

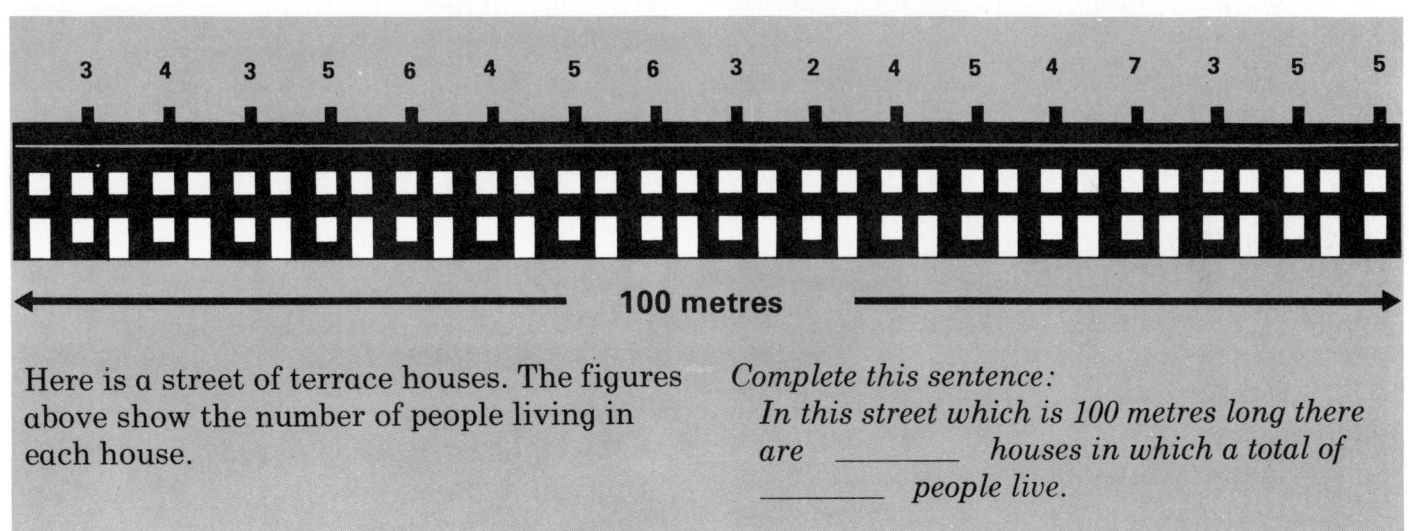

| 3 | 4 | 3 | 5 | 6 | 4 | 5 | 6 | 3 | 2 | 4 | 5 | 4 | 7 | 3 | 5 | 5 |

100 metres

Here is a street of terrace houses. The figures above show the number of people living in each house.

Complete this sentence:
In this street which is 100 metres long there are _____ houses in which a total of _____ people live.

This map shows a piece of land 100 metres square (1 hectare). The map shows each house, garden and backyard. Pavements and verges are also shown.

Complete this sentence:
   In this area of 10,000 square metres there are ———— houses.

   One house looks like this ▯ or this ▯ .

How does this number compare with the number of semis on page 5?

If four people lived in each of these houses, how many people would be living on this hectare of land?

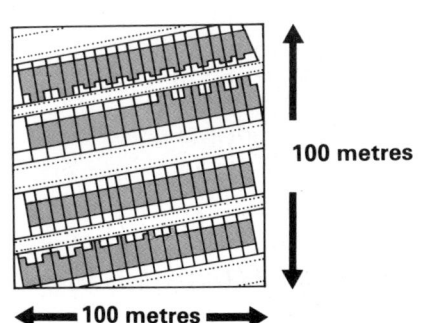

100 metres

◀— 100 metres —▶

Houses in the neighbourhood—detached

Look back to page 2 and find where the Newell family lives.

Yes, they live in the big detached house that backs on to the school field. In fact the school is built in what were once the grounds of this large house. The Newells do not live there by themselves because the big house has been divided into four flats, each one lived in by a different family.

Write a sentence under each of these headings, comparing this house with one of the semi-detached houses on page 4:
> *Age*
> *Size*
> *Size of the garden*
> *Building materials—walls, roof, windows*
> *Extra detail added to the house*

How was this house made to look imposing and grand? Draw some of the building details. Do you think there will be many other houses exactly like this one?
Is this house the same as the semi in any ways? Why have so many houses like this one been divided into a number of flats?

Here is another map showing a piece of land 100 metres square (1 hectare). The houses here are all detached houses.

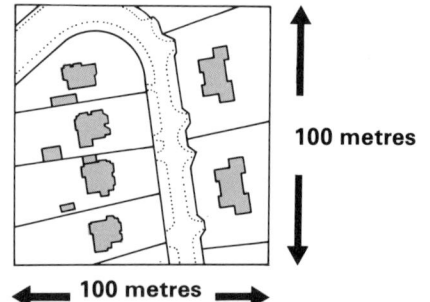

100 metres

100 metres

Complete this sentence:
> *In this area of 10,000 square metres there are _____ houses.*
If four people live in each house how many people live on this hectare of land?

Here is a street of detached houses. It is the same length as the street on page 5.

How many houses are there in this street? If once upon a time eight people lived in each house, how many lived here altogether?

If each of these houses has now been divided into three flats, how many homes are there altogether now?
If four people live in each flat, how many people live here altogether now?

100 metres

Other homes—flats

From time to time Julie and Richard Pickwick go to visit their cousins who live in another part of town. The visit is quite an adventure because their cousins live on the seventh floor of this block of flats.

Describe the shape of the walls and roof.
What building materials seem to have been used to build them?
How many floors are there altogether?
If each floor is 2½m high, what is the total height of the block?
How many times higher is this block than the semi-detached houses on page 4?

If we were looking down on this block from the air it would look like this:

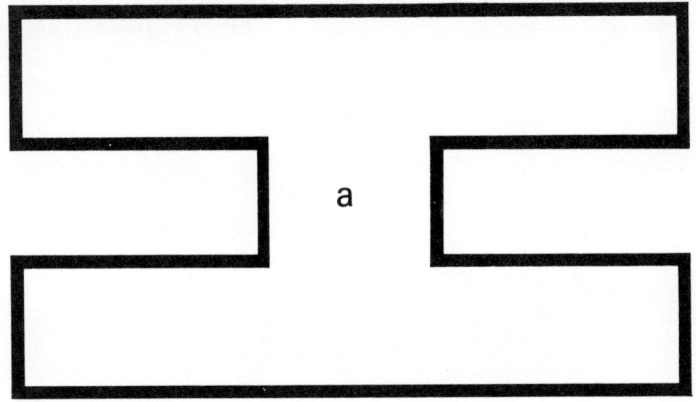

The centre part (a) is used for lifts, stairs, waste disposal chutes and so on. The two sides of the H are divided into three flats each. In other words, there are six flats on each floor.

Study the photograph and see if you can see how the flats are arranged.
How many flats are there in the whole building?
If each flat has a family of three in it, how many people live in the whole building?
How does this compare with a row of terrace houses (page 7)?

Such blocks as this usually have a lot of open space left around them—in fact there may be only one such block in a street of 100 metres.

Can you think of any good reasons why blocks like this are built with lots of space around them?

Here is another piece of map showing an area of land 100 metres square (1 hectare).
The buildings on it are two blocks of flats each with 47 flats.

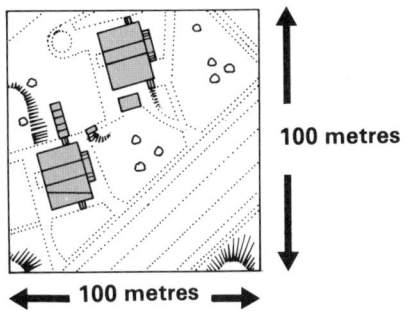

100 metres

100 metres

Complete this sentence:
    In this area of 10,000 square metres there are _____ *flats.*
If four people live in each flat how many people live on this hectare of land?

Write a short story about living in a high block of flats.

At the building site

Building sites are interesting —but dangerous—places. Tersame Bhogal has kept a diary of what happened when houses were built across the road from his home (see pages 2 and 3).

When you have read Tersame's diary answer these questions:

1 When did they start building these houses? When was the brickwork of the house opposite to Tersame's nearly finished? Use a calendar to help you find out how long it took to build the house.

2 Here are some of the people who help to build a house: bricklayer; joiner; tiler; plasterer; electrician; plumber.
For each one, find out: what he does; the main tools he uses; the building materials

April
10 Monday
Men with measuring instruments, tapes, poles and pegs have marked out the house plots. They said they were surveyors.

12 Wednesday
Trenches being dug everywhere. What for?

13 Thursday
I know! They are laying water pipes and drains.

18 Tuesday
More men have arrived to put in electric cables.

27 Thursday
Men laying water pipes finished but still more men laying gas pipes. Mud everywhere, what a mess!

May
8 Monday
Now they've really started on the house opposite. Foundation trenches have been dug and filled with concrete.

15 Monday
Concrete hard. Brickies have built up the walls to just above ground level and stopped.

he uses in the house; which parts of the house he is mainly concerned with.

3 Help Tersame by finding out what a **damp course** is made of and why it is necessary to have one.

4 Find out why houses have a **cavity wall**.

5 Make a list of all the materials used in the building of a house—the pictures above will help you. Find out how bricks are made and why one side of them is hollowed out. Which of the materials used was once a living thing?

6 Can you find the "recipe" for making cement?

7 Here are some common words used in the building of houses; find out what they refer to and identify them on the pictures below: rafters; eaves; scaffolding; joists; casement; ridge; jamb.

19 Friday
See why they stopped — had to put down a concrete floor. Done that today.

25 Thursday
Brickies busy again. Laid down a "damp course" on the wall and then went on building up. Wonder what a damp course is for?

29 Monday
House now up to bedroom level with window and door frames in. See that walls are two thicknesses with a gap between. The men call it a "cavity wall."

31 Wednesday
House now covered in scaffolding so that work can go on higher up.

June
5 Monday
Brickies finished

8 Thursday
What a racket! Joiners putting on the roof. Learnt some new words - beam, rafters, joists and purlins.

12 Monday
Tilers don't take long to put felt and tiles on the roof.

19 Monday
Glass being put in the windows while men tidy-up outside and flatten the garden. Only plasterer to come now.

11

The neighbourhood map

Here is a picture of the area where the Pickwicks live. You have seen it before. Below is a map of the same area.

Look closely at the map and picture. See if you can find the same features on both.

Ask your teacher for a copy of the map, or trace one for yourself. Use the map to do these things.

1 *Mark with an initial letter where each of the families we have heard about lives.*

2 *Mark and name one example of each of the following:*

> *footpath*
> *farm track*
> *valley*
> *country lane*
> *street*
> *semi-detached house*
> *detached house*
> *row of terrace houses*
> *factory*
> *school*
> *church*
> *park*
> *field*
> *row of shops*

You will have to do this work very carefully so that it is not too untidy.

Describe some of the patterns you can find on the map or picture to your neighbour in class.

See if he or she can point to what you have described.

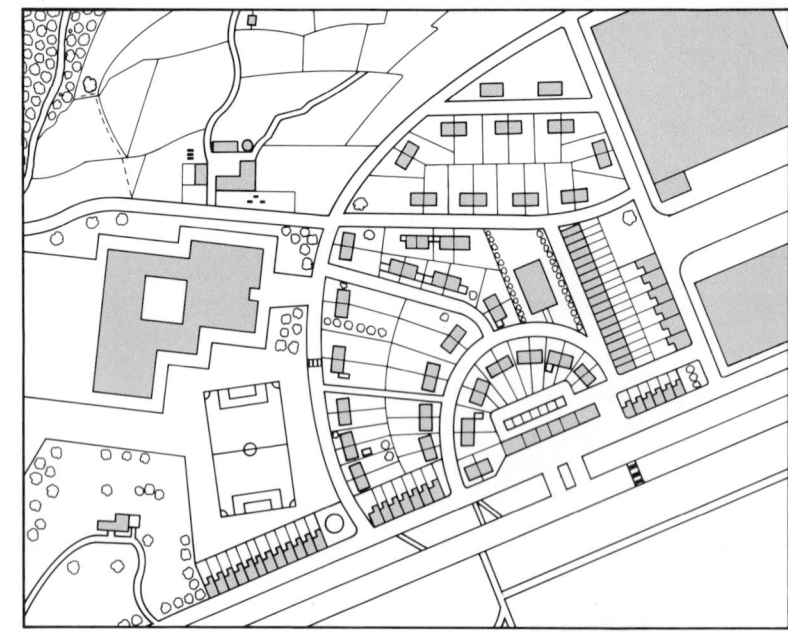

Another neighbourhood

Hans Schmidt lives in a village called St Goar. It is in Germany, by the side of the great River Rhine. The village is about halfway between two towns, Koblenz and Bingen.
Can you find these towns in your atlas?
Because the village is fairly small the whole of the village is Hans Schmidt's neighbourhood.
Look carefully at the map and photograph.

Photograph of St Goar taken from the castle ▶
(the dashed line on the map shows the area covered by the photo).

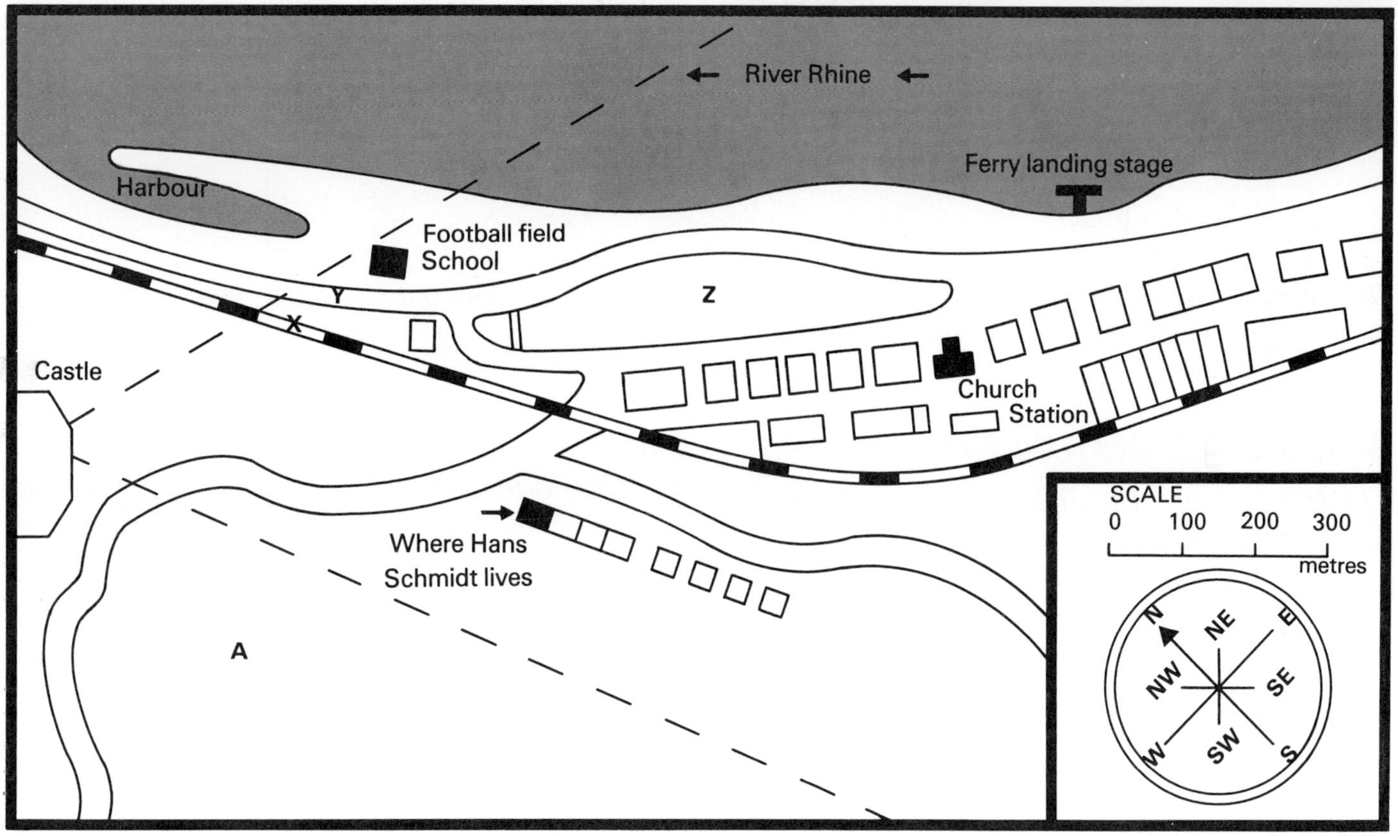

Look at X and Y on the map. Now look at the photograph. Which is the road, and which the railway?
Now look at Z and A. At which of these places do you find trees on steep ground, and where do you find buildings?

If Hans wanted to go from his house to some of the places in the neighbourhood he would walk because the distances are small.

What direction would he take, if he could walk in a straight line, to get to the following places from his home:

   to school;

   to the castle;

   to the ferry?

Which of these statements is true?
   The harbour is north, north west of Hans' house.
   The river runs in a south east to north west direction.
   Hans' road runs in a south east to north west direction.

WHAT LIES TO THE SOUTH OF HANS' HOUSE?

WHAT LIES TO THE WEST OF THE HOUSE?

Getting to school

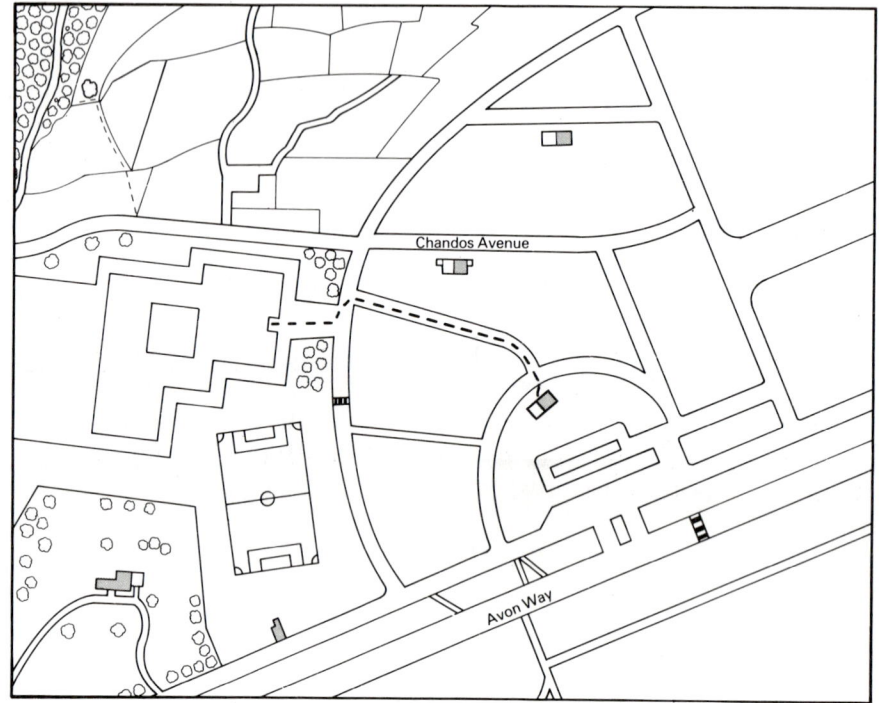

This map shows Julie's route to school. *Can you find her house, the school and her route?*

Imagine a line going straight from Julie's house to school. This is the **direct** distance.

Which is further—the direct route (as the crow flies) or the route Julie takes?

Why does she have to take this longer route?

*Name some of the things which make her change direction. We call this **making a detour**.*

On a copy of the map draw the direct route and the actual walking route, from home to school, of the other children.

Now put the correct name in these sentences:

_____ lives closest to the school, as the crow flies.

_____ lives furthest from the school, as the crow flies.

Make a list to show how long each of their journeys would be if they could travel as the crow flies. Start with the shortest and finish with the longest.

_____ has the shortest actual walk to school.

_____ has the longest walk to school.

Now make another list to show how long each of the walking journeys of the children is. Start with the shortest and finish with the longest.

Are the two lists exactly the same? If not, say why you think they are different.

PUZZLE PUZZLE

WHO LIVES CLOSE TO SCHOOL BUT HAS A ROUNDABOUT WALK TO GET TO SCHOOL?

WHO LIVES A LONG WAY FROM SCHOOL BUT HAS A FAIRLY DIRECT ROUTE TO GET THERE?

You now have a map which shows several journeys to school.

Put a number 1 on each bit of route which is only used by one person. Put a number 2 on any stretch of route used by two people. Put a 3 for a route used by three people and so on.

Which stretch of route is used by most people?

As you have seen on the map opposite, all these children walk to school.
Some of their classmates come to school on the bus or on bicycles. A few of them are brought to school in their parents' cars.

Julie and Sharmilla went round the class asking each child in turn:
"How did you come to school today?"

and then:
"How long does it take you to get to school?"

They made a simple chart to show this information. *Can you make a chart which would help you to collect this information from your classmates? Try it and see what information you get.*

I'll give you a clue . . .

	Julie	Sharmilla	Jane	Robert	Neil	Richard	Pete
Walk							
Bus							

From the information Julie and Sharmilla were able to collect they drew a chart like this one, with some help from their teacher.

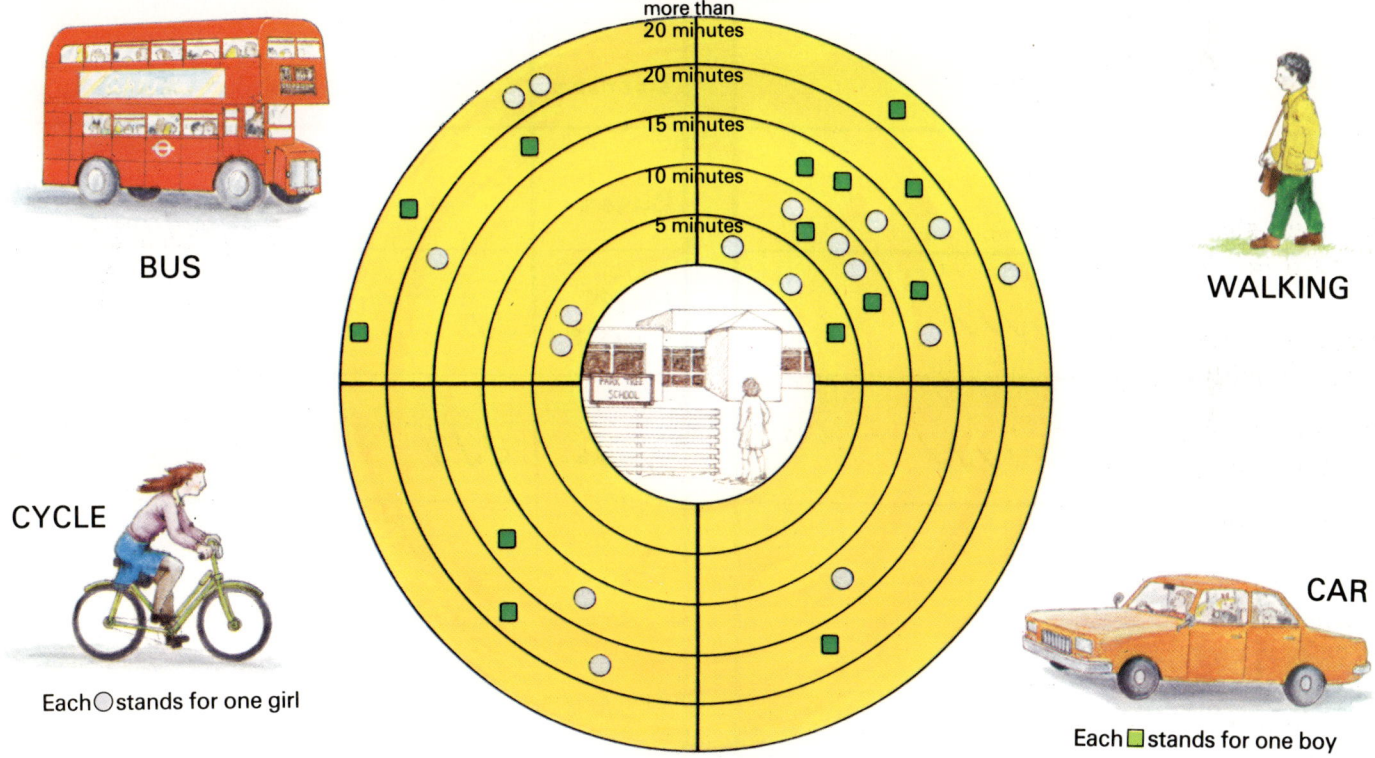

BUS

CYCLE

Each ◯ stands for one girl

more than
20 minutes

20 minutes

15 minutes

10 minutes

5 minutes

WALKING

CAR

Each ▢ stands for one boy

Look closely at the chart.
How many children walk to school?
How many come by car?
How many come by bike?
How many come by bus?

Which is the most popular way of travelling to school?

Which is the least popular?
How many children take more than 15 minutes to get to school?
How many take less than five minutes?
Copy and complete this table:

How many . . .	Boys walk	Boys go by bus	Girls walk	Girls go by bus	Girls take 10 mins or more?	Boys take 10 mins or more?

Counting traffic

One morning, for ten minutes, Ian Kirkpatrick and Tim Cooper counted the traffic passing along two of the roads in their neighbourhood, Avon Way and Chandos Avenue. They did it by making charts like those below, clipped to pieces of hardboard.

As each vehicle passed them they put a tick in the correct column, making a tally chart.

You can see what the two charts looked like. Ian and Tim were surprised to see how different the two were.

A CLIP BOARD IS EASY TO MAKE

PAPER CLIP

CHART

HARDBOARD OR STIFF CARD

YOU COULD COVER IT WITH A PLASTIC BAG IN CASE OF RAIN !

Cars	✓✓✓✓✓✓✓✓✓✓✓ ✓✓✓✓✓ ✓✓ ✓ ✓✓✓✓
Lorries	✓✓✓✓✓✓
Buses	✓✓✓✓
Motor Cycles	✓✓✓✓✓✓ ✓✓✓✓
Vans	✓✓✓ ✓✓✓✓✓✓✓
Bikes	✓✓✓
Others	✓

Cars	✓✓✓✓✓
Lorries	
Buses	
Motor Cycles	✓✓
Vans	✓✓✓
Bikes	✓✓
Others	

Find the two roads on the map on page 14. Draw column graphs to show how much traffic there was on the two roads.
Which of the two charts was made on Avon Way?
Which types of vehicle did not pass along Chandos Avenue?
Why do you think this is so?

These traffic counts were made between 10.50 and 11.00am on a weekday.

How might the number and type of vehicles have been different if the count had been taken for ten minutes between 8.00 and 9.00am on a Sunday? Or on a weekday at the same time?

All the vehicles are making journeys for a reason.

Can you think of some of the possible reasons for the journeys of:
    cars?
    lorries?

Different roads

Tim and Ian were both very interested in vehicles. They found out that different roads carry different types and numbers of vehicles. This made them think about other ways in which roads of all kinds are different. They decided to make this chart to try to plot some of these differences. They have filled in the row for the main road.

Can you finish the chart for them? Do so by looking at the roads in your own area.

Can you think of any other information you could collect to bring out the similarities and differences between the roads?

What about colours, language, wild life, litter *in the roads?*

Type of road	Main		
How wide it is	10 metres		
What its surface is made of	Tarmac		
What traffic uses it people walking			
cyclists			
cars	✓		
vans	✓		
lorries	✓		
buses	✓		

How fast is the traffic moving
   5. Very fast
   4. Fairly fast
   3. Normally
   2. Quite slow
   1. Very slow
	5		

How much traffic
   A. Heavy
   B. Medium
   C. Light
	A		

What 'furniture' is there in the road or street	Lights, traffic signs		

"Going to school"—a game

Play this game with a partner.

The hexagons are:

red for houses and school

green for park and playing fields

brown for road and demolition area.

You will need some counters (plastic ones are best or you may use small pieces of paper).

Rules

The object of the game is to get from your home (one of the hexagons numbered 1 to 8) to school as quickly as possible (ie using the least number of counters).

1 The first player chooses a hexagon 1–8; the second player then chooses one of the remaining hexagons.

2 Each player, in turn, then puts one counter over a hexagon to build up a routeway from home to school.

3 You may only cross the major road at the zebra crossing.

4 You cannot go through houses.

5 You can cross the park, the demolition area and the school playing fields but must put two counters (ie two turns) on each hexagon you cross in those areas.

6 Each hexagon may be occupied by more than one player's counter.

When you finally reach school leave your counters where they are and count up how many you have used in getting to school.

Now answer these questions.

- *Describe briefly the pattern of your own route.*
- *Say how your friend's route was different from yours.*
- *What barriers or obstacles did you have to avoid when planning your route?*
- *Did you use the same hexagons as your partner on any occasion? Why?*
- *Which are the least busy parts of the routeway on the map? Why?*
- *Which are likely to be the busiest parts of the routeways on the map? Why?*
- *Where do problems arise on your journey? How are they solved?*

I'M GOING TO TRY THE GAME AGAIN! AND SEE IF I CAN IMPROVE MY SCORE!

LEAVE THE COUNTERS WHERE THEY ARE.

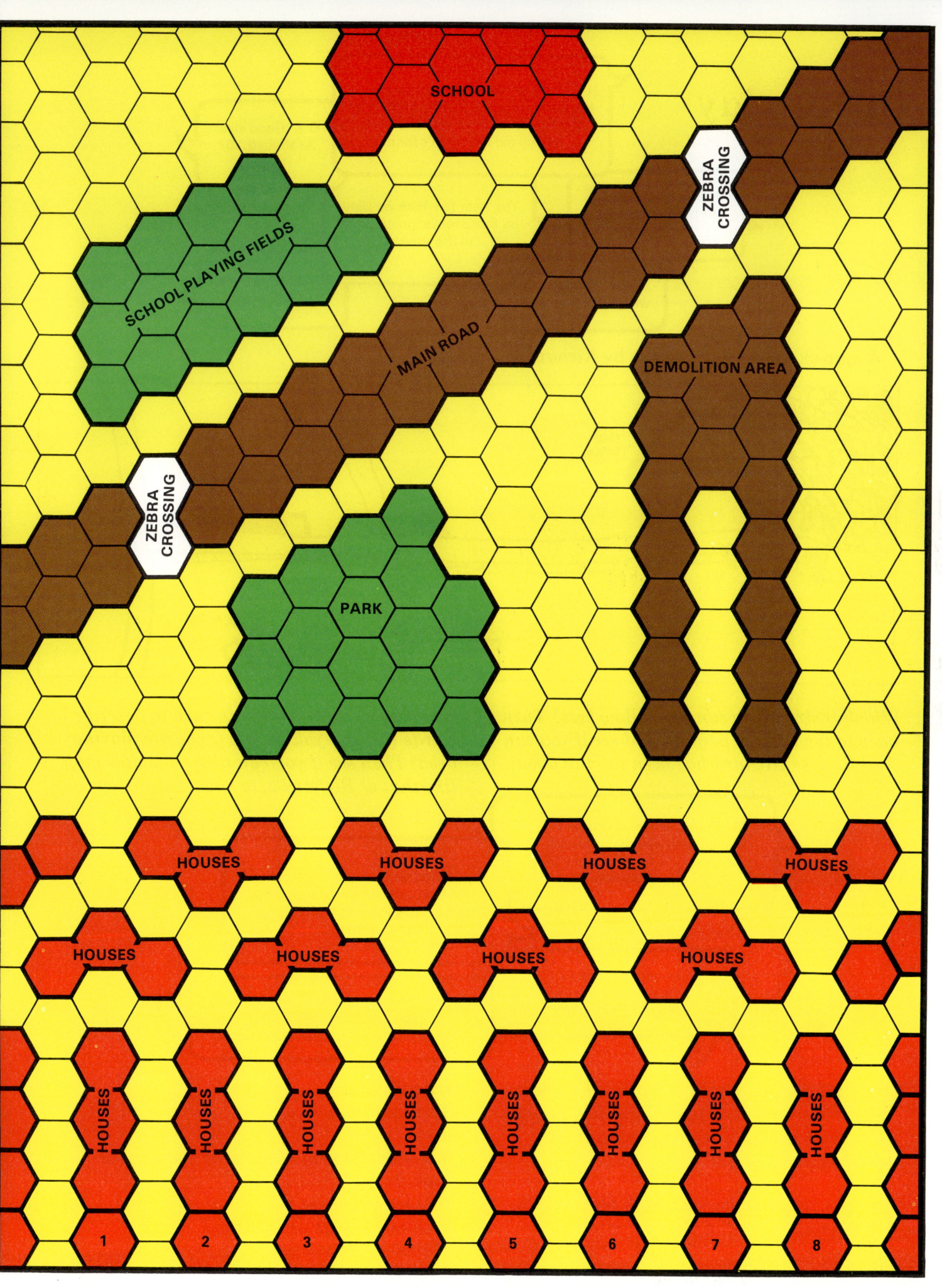

Off to play

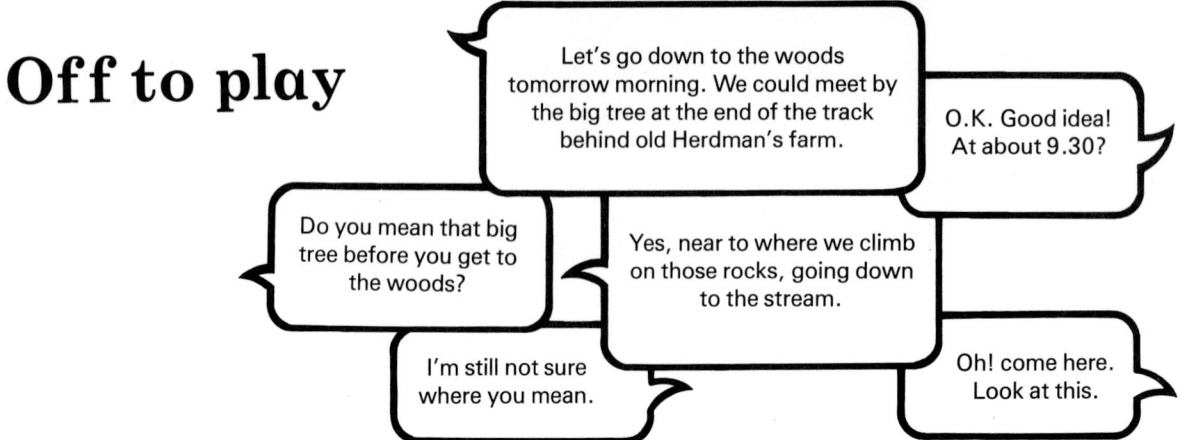

A map sketched out quickly by Richard.

Which instructions can you follow best? Turn back to the map on page 12 and see if you can find the tree Richard has been talking about.

Working in pairs, take it in turn to describe in words the way you go to a favourite playing area. Then see if you can draw a simple map, like that of Richard's, to show the same route.

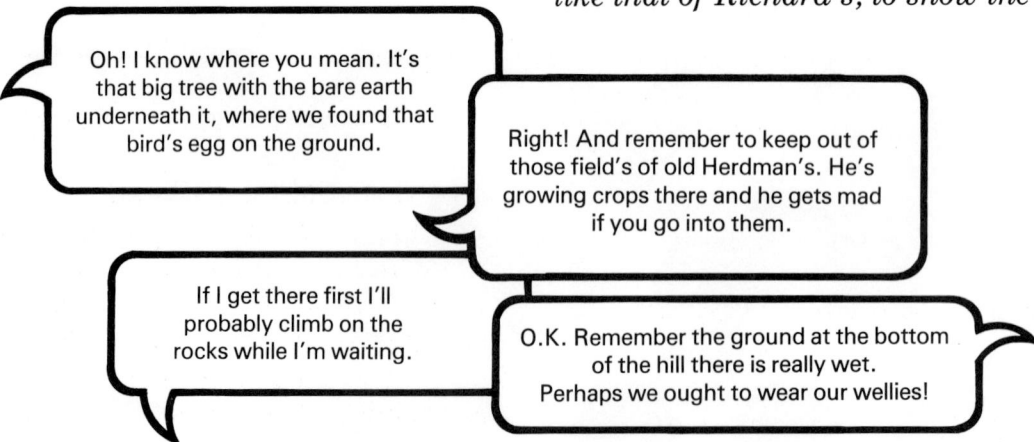

The children have told us quite a lot about this area where they play. They have been using words which describe what their **environment** is like.

Can you list some words which best describe:
The environment of your playground at school?
The environment of your favourite playing area?
The environment of the area round your home?
The environment of another place you've been to (seaside or country)?

20

*Look again at the map on page 12. Find the homes of the children who have arranged to meet by the tree: Richard, Tim, Tersame, Sandra and Jane. Now try to find (or **locate**) the big tree behind the farm. Here is part of that map redrawn for you.*

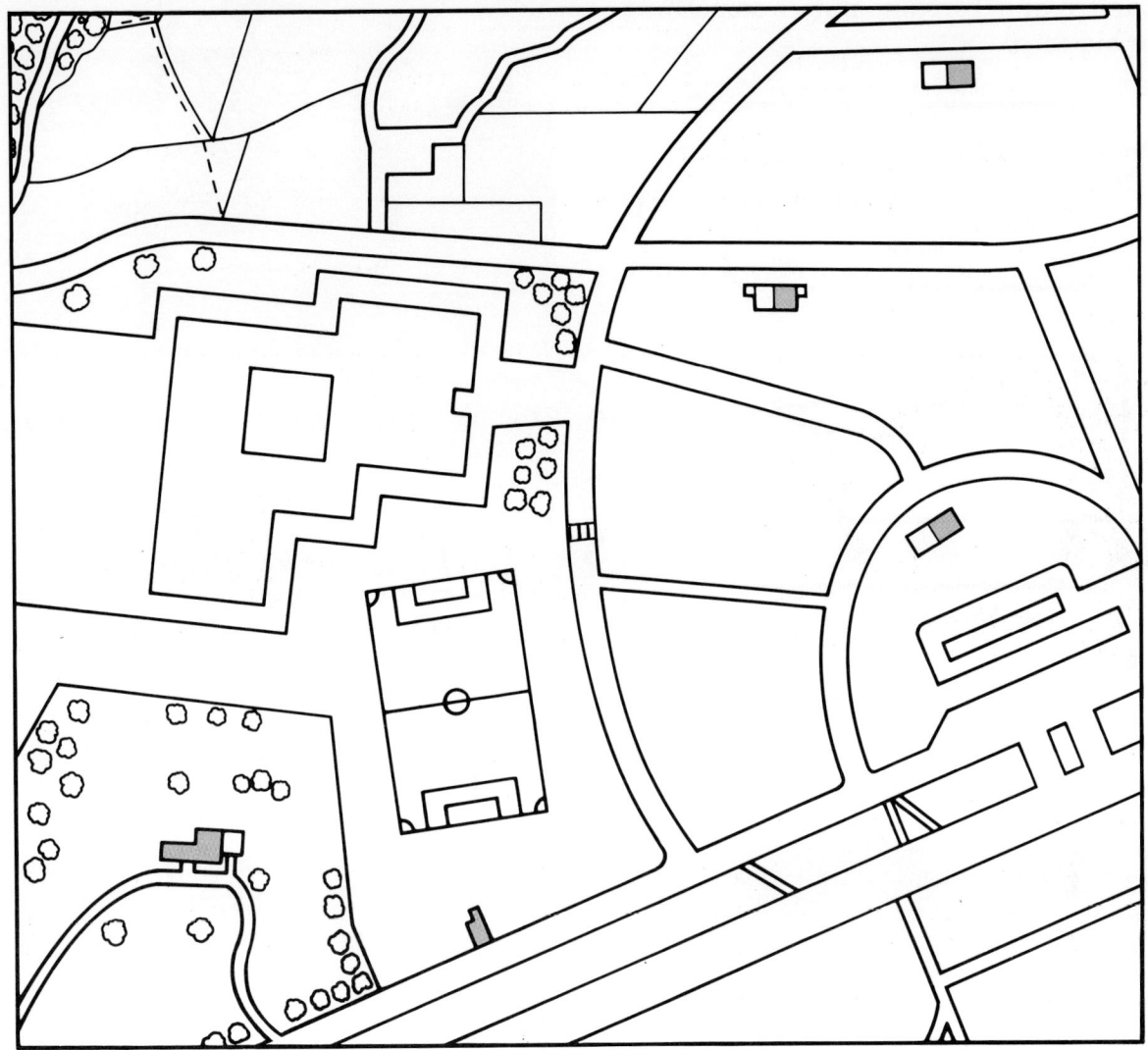

If all the children left home to go to the tree at exactly the same time, who would get there first? Why?
Who would be the last to arrive?
Why?
Is it likely that they would all leave at exactly the same time?
Why?
Which of the kids could take a short cut?
Describe the way he or she would go.
Draw two simple maps, one to show the long journey and one the short cut. Is the short cut very much shorter?

Using the map on page 3 and the picture on page 2, describe as accurately as you can the route followed by one of the children.

When the children get home Sandra's mum says that their garage is not going to be used for a while as the man who rented it has left. She says the kids can use it as a den or a headquarters. Sandra thinks that is a great idea and she decides to run round to each of her friends in turn to tell them the news.

Trace the map above and then plot the route Sandra will run if she visits all her friends in turn.

As she is running, she thinks it would be a good idea to take a different route home.
Can you plot another route on your tracing?

Meeting at the tree

While they are waiting for the others to arrive, Sandra and Tersame notice something about the big tree.

> It's peculiar isn't it? It stands on its own! There's this big patch of bare ground underneath it too!

> I wonder why it is bare?

> There are some more trees over by the factories, but I can't remember whether they have bare ground or not.

YOU'VE STARTED ME THINKING NOW! HOW MANY EXPLANATIONS CAN YOU THINK OF? HERE ARE SOME OF MINE... SOMEONE'S DUG UP THE GRASS... SOMEONE'S PUT WEEDKILLER ROUND THE TREE... THE TREE ROOTS ARE CHOKING THE GRASS... GRASS WON'T GROW BECAUSE OF THE TREE'S SHADE.... THE SOIL IS DIFFERENT....

Do you know of any trees near to where you live which have these areas of bare ground? What other explanations might there be? Can you think of any ways you might be able to test which of these ideas is best?

Draw an outline of the tree. It has a very distinctive shape. This shape often helps us to find out what type (or species) of tree it is. *Which of these shapes does it most closely resemble?*

Richard suggests that one of the things the "gang" could do is to collect things of interest while they are out in the woods. "We could then have our own sort of museum back in Sandra's garage."
"Shall we start by taking back a leaf and a twig from this tree so we can find out from my *Observer's Book* what sort of tree it is?"

You could collect the leaves and twigs from different trees (and draw outlines of them) so that you can find which trees grow near your home.

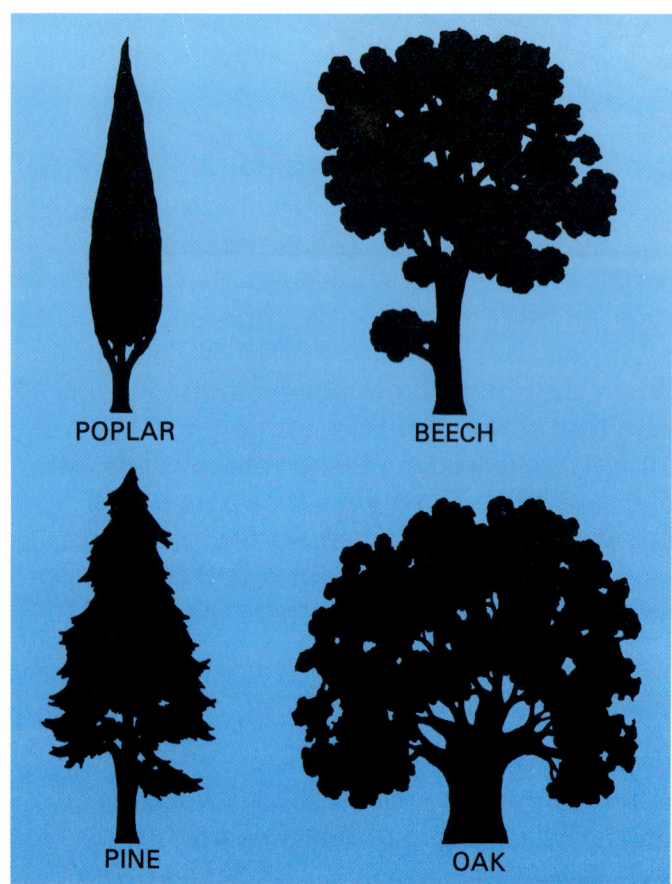

POPLAR   BEECH

PINE   OAK

Still waiting, looking around them the kids notice a number of insects crawling on the bark of the tree. As they look closer they then notice that there are some caterpillars hanging from some of the leaves. Higher up in the tree they see a bird's nest in the fork of a branch. Just then a larger bird settles on a branch for a moment, pecks at something, and then flies away.

"Its amazing how much life there is in and around a tree isn't it?" Jane comments. "Come to think of it, this tree is almost like a separate little world, with insects and birds and things living in it . . . hey! Do you remember that super coloured picture we found in that children's encyclopaedia about the world of the tree?"

"No, I don't remember it too well, but perhaps we could draw a big picture from it to put up on the garage wall. It could go by the side of our twigs and leaves."

The picture they were thinking about is shown below. The big arrows show the things which a tree needs in order to grow and survive. The dotted arrows show some of the things which may come from the tree. Some of the things which happen in the tree are printed in the picture.

Draw a similar diagram for yourself but see if you can think of other things to add to it. Have a look at a tree near you. Stand quietly by it. Watch. Listen. This might help you to get more information for your diagram.

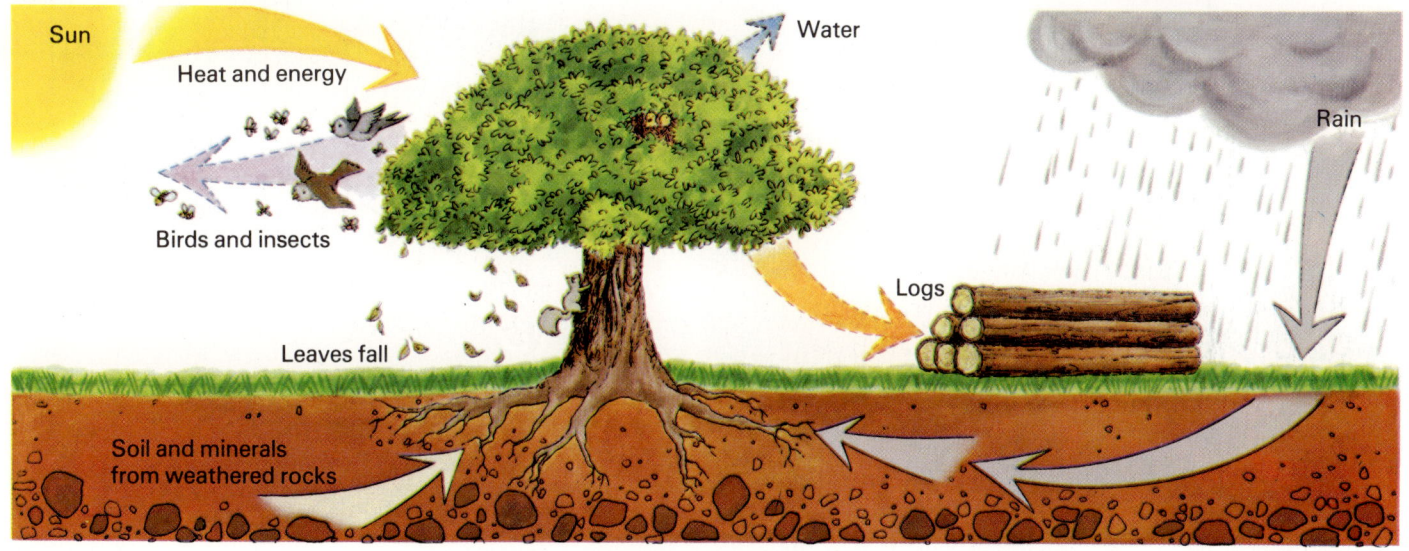

The bird which landed on the tree for a moment and then flew off probably came for something to eat. In nature you find that one creature feeds off another . . . what we have just seen is probably:

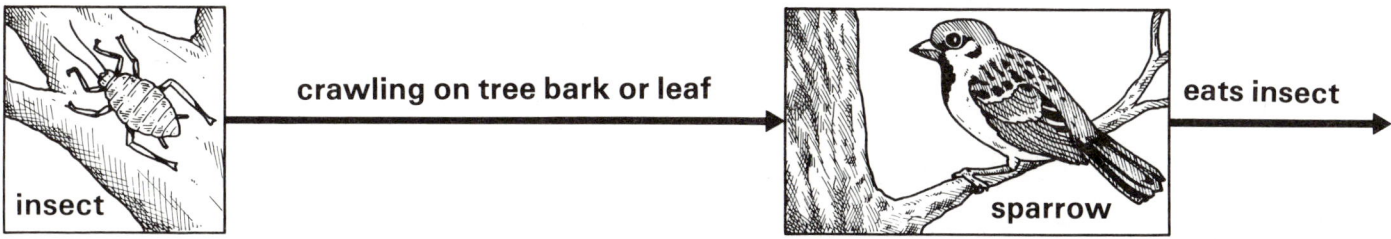

Can you think of any creatures which feed off others? Make a simple diagram following this pattern: this is known as a **food chain.**

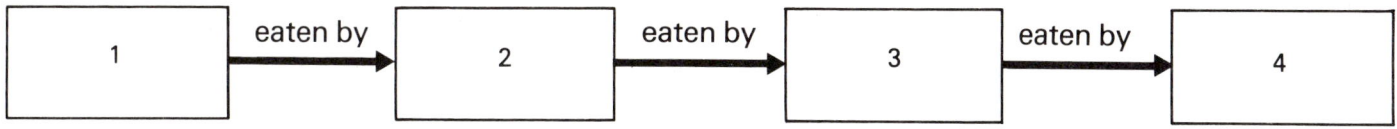

23

Through the woods

When all the children have arrived at the tree they decide to go straight down to the stream.

"Let's walk in an absolutely straight line," says Richard.

"But you know we have to go over the rocks and through the bog," replies Tim.

'We'll try it anyway."

As the children go they chatter to each other. This drawing shows the route they took as they walked in a straight line. It is like taking a slice across the hillside. Such a drawing is called a **section**.

You can see what they said about each part of the walk.

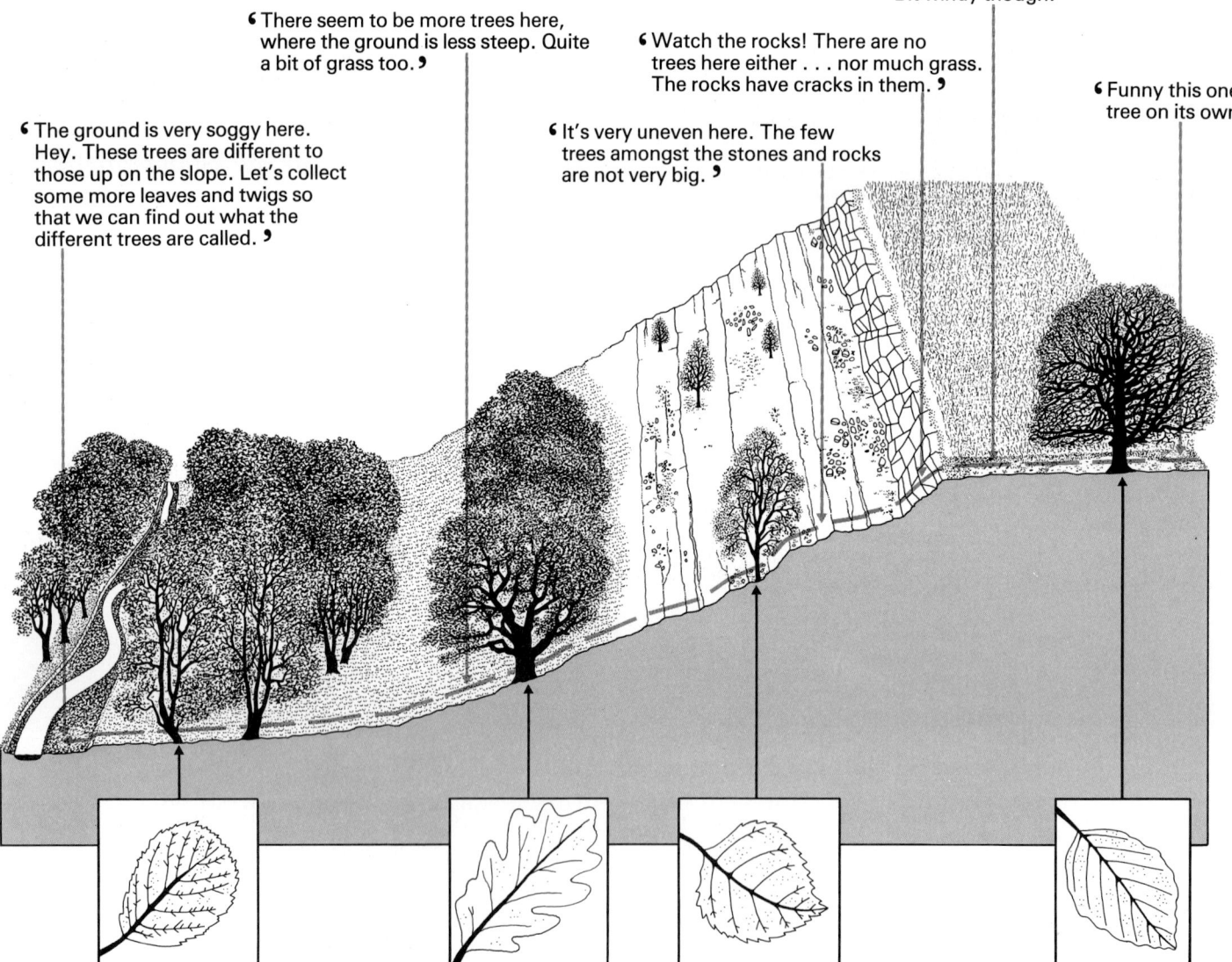

'There seem to be more trees here, where the ground is less steep. Quite a bit of grass too.'

'The ground is very soggy here. Hey. These trees are different to those up on the slope. Let's collect some more leaves and twigs so that we can find out what the different trees are called.'

'Watch the rocks! There are no trees here either . . . nor much grass. The rocks have cracks in them.'

'It's very uneven here. The few trees amongst the stones and rocks are not very big.'

'Easy walking here — it's so flat. Bit windy though.'

'Funny this one tree on its own.'

These are the leaves they collected. *Can you find which trees they come from?*

Copy this section into your books. Underneath the section write (as small as possible) the words from this list which best describe the kids' walk down through the woods:

flat, uneven, rocky,
steep, windy, boggy.

Try to write the words in the right place on the section.

Put a letter S where you think it might be sheltered from the wind; an R where you might find rocks and boulders; a C where there might be most trees to climb.

24

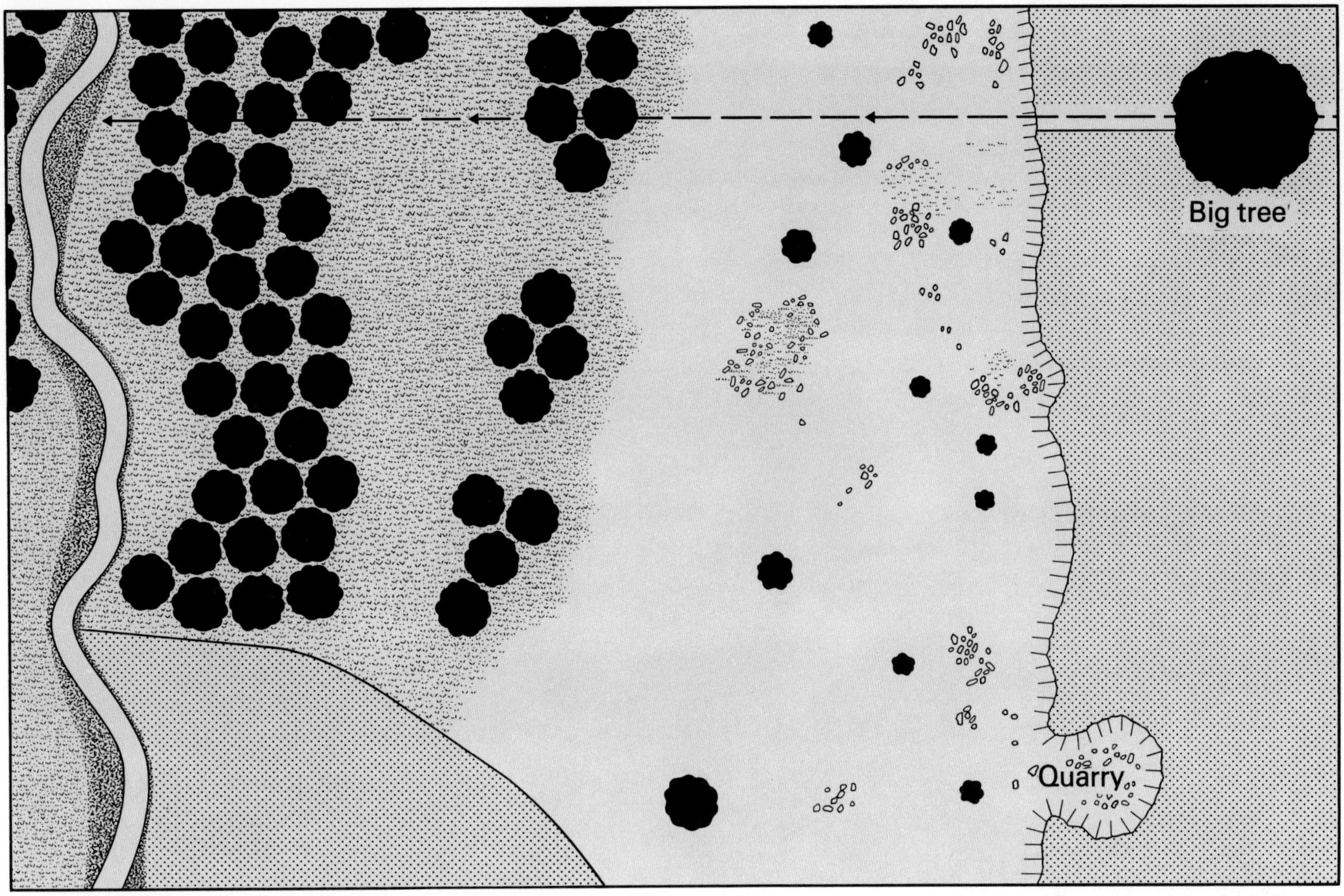

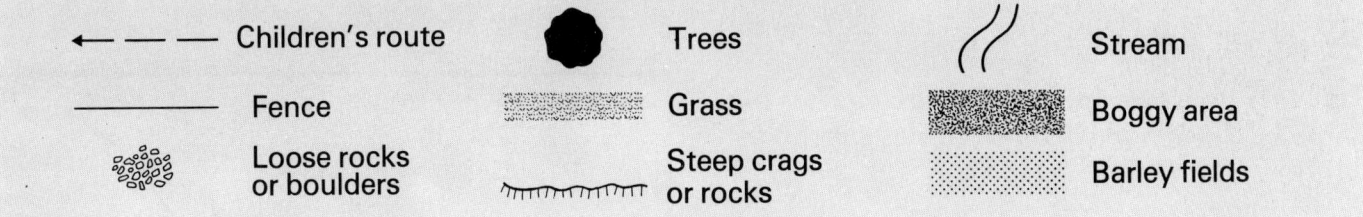

Look carefully at this map. It shows the route taken by the kids as they made their way down to the stream. Use this "key" to help you to identify things on the map:

← – – – –	Children's route	●	Trees	∫∫	Stream
——————	Fence	░░░	Grass	▓▓	Boggy area
⁙	Loose rocks or boulders	⌄⌄⌄⌄	Steep crags or rocks	∷∷	Barley fields

There are a number of different patterns on this map.

Place a sheet of tracing paper over it and then mark on the tracing paper the following patterns. Choose your own way of showing them:

- ●*A line pattern*
- ●*A straight line pattern*
- ●*A bending line pattern*
- ●*Clusters of things*
- ●*A patch of woodland*
- ●*A patch of grassland*
- ●*Trees dotted about*
- ●*The semi-circular pattern of the quarry*

Also use your tracing paper to show which areas have most trees, by marking on the paper:

an area with no trees;
another with few trees;
one with many trees.

Do you find most trees near the water or on the hill top?
Why do you think this may be?

Trees are often found in different places. *Look at the trees around your school or home. Where are they found? Can you suggest why?*

Down by the stream

Here you can see the children playing by the stream. The words on the picture are words they have used to describe what it is like.

Copy this map into your book, making it as big as you can. Then mark on your map where the children found:

 deep water
 shallow water
 rough water
 sand and pebbles
 falling soil
 wet ground
 dry ground

Use colours or signs rather than words to show these on your map.

You can also see the path followed by a paper boat they floated.

Mark this on your map too.
Why do you think Sandra and Tim chose to cross the stream at this point?

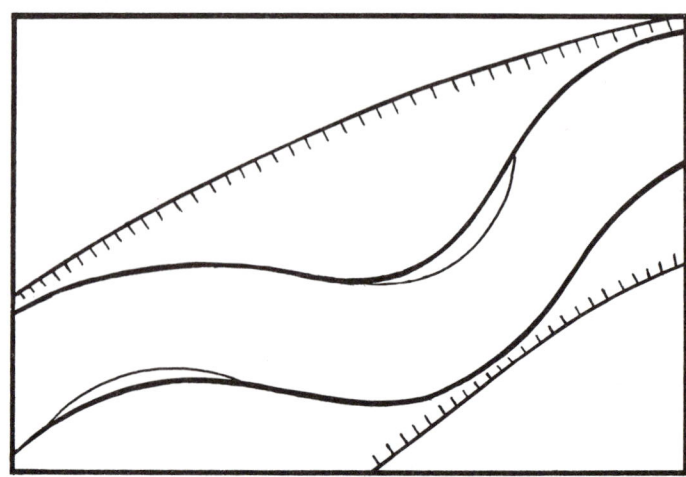

See if you can visit your local stream, perhaps with your class or with some of your friends. Look closely at it. Does it have deep and shallow areas? Rough and calm water? How does it differ from the stretch of stream the kids play in, in this book?

On the rocks

These photographs were taken by Jane's dad. They show the rocks the children play on when they go down to the woods. There are quite a few blocks of stone and boulders lying around and the kids sometimes climb and play on these. The rock faces such as those shown in the photos are usually too steep for them to climb safely.

Look carefully at the photographs and describe the rocks. Use some of these words:
 steep,
 craggy,
 boulders,
 cracks,
 joints,
 high.
Use this diagram to find out what the photograph shows.

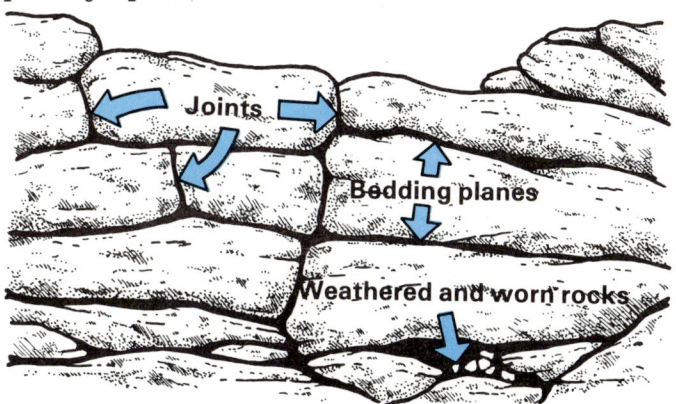

Joints

Bedding planes

Weathered and worn rocks

The children say the rock is very rough to touch. It is sandy and has gritty bits in it. It is a rock called a sandstone. Sandstones are sometimes harder than other rocks and so stand out as hills or crags like these.

Sometimes sandstones are quarried by man because the stone can be used for building, or it can be crushed and turned into sand.
Can you find the old quarry on the map on page 25?

Suppose some rain fell on to the rocks in photo A. How do you think it would drain away?
It would probably follow the joints and cracks. As it moved over the rocks it might begin to wear them away. This is called **erosion.** The children notice quite a lot of sand at the foot of these cliffs. It has probably been carried there by rainwater running over the sandstone.

See if you can find any rocks near where you live. Make a collection in the classroom. Describe each of them carefully. Which is the hardest? Which is the softest?

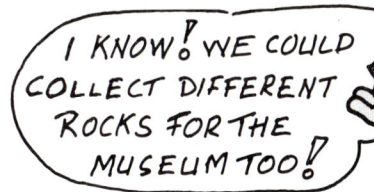

I KNOW! WE COULD COLLECT DIFFERENT ROCKS FOR THE MUSEUM TOO!

"Playing in the park"—a game

Sometimes, instead of going down to the woods to play, the children and often their families too, go to the park to play.

Do you have a park near you? What sort of things do you play at in the park? Are there any swings or roundabouts?

Imagine that you are visiting this park for the first time. You want to have a turn on everything. Plan your route round the playground so that you take the least number of hexagons, but at the same time visit all the playthings.

Compare your route with that of your friends or partners. Which is the shortest? Next time you visit the park a new fence has been put up between points X and Y. You may now have to find a new route. Does this barrier make your route shorter or longer?

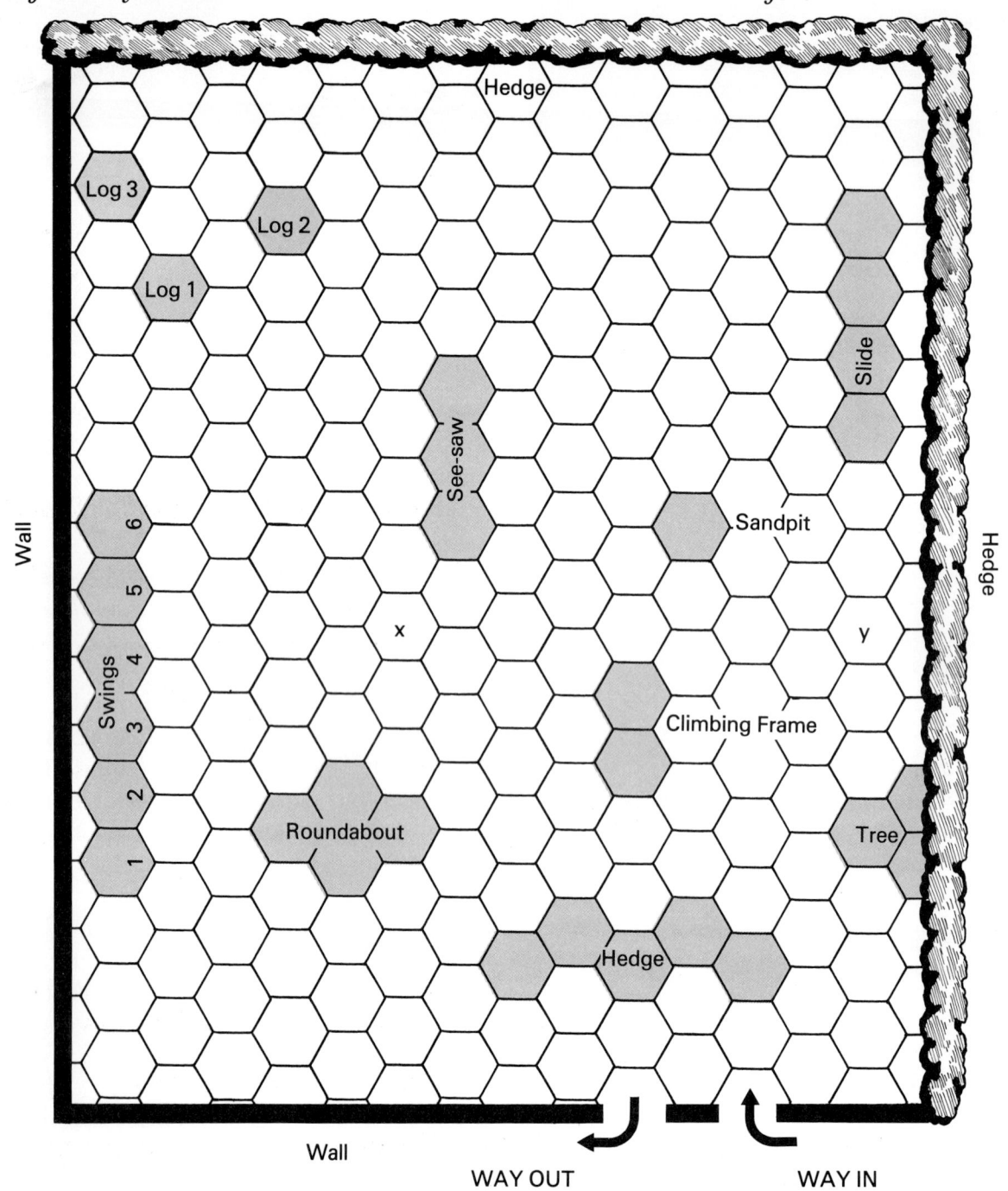

Planning the playground

Here is a plan view of an area of ground which a town council has decided will be used to provide a new playground.

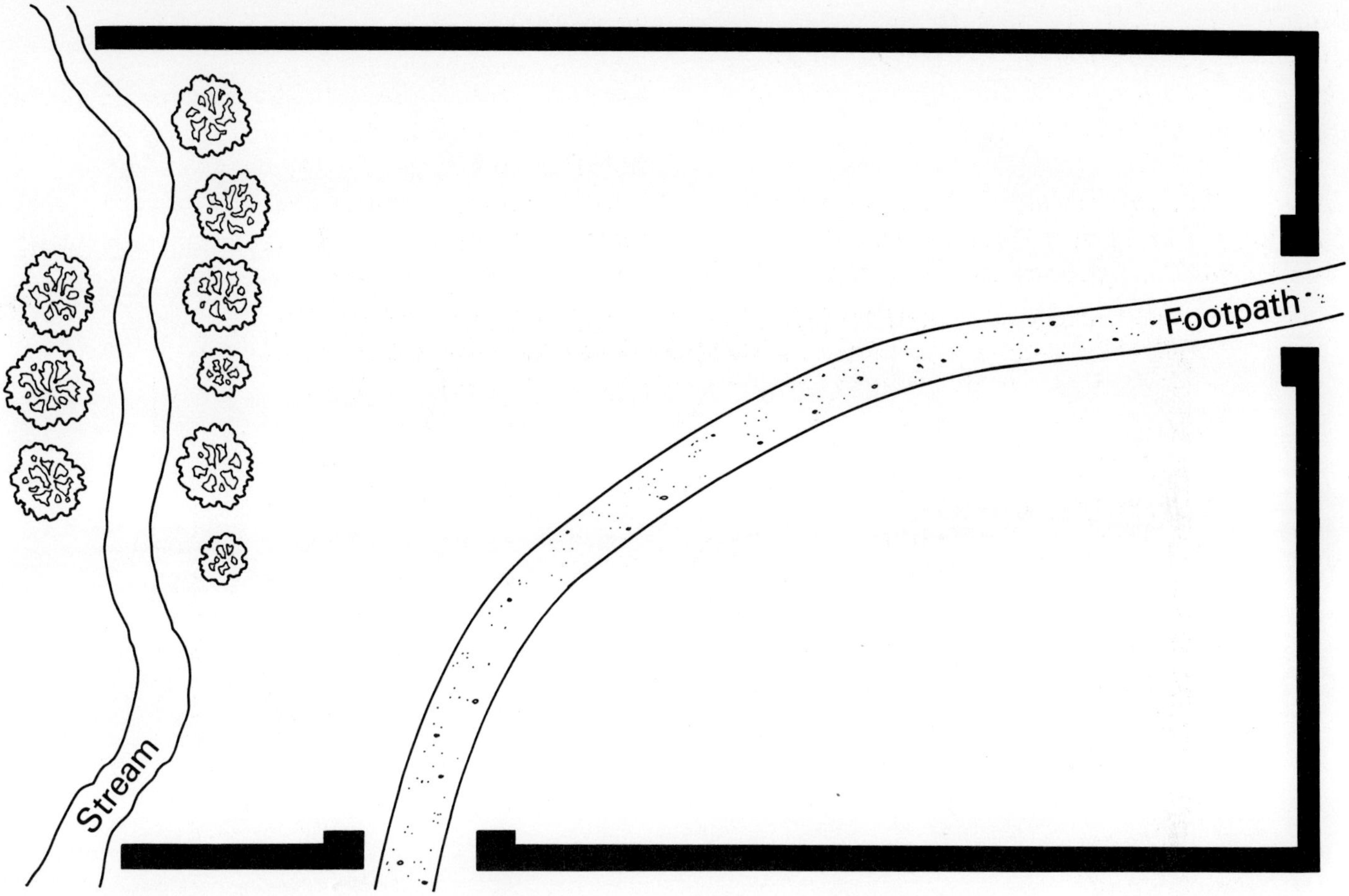

Footpath

Stream

Copy this plan into your book and become a planner for a while by deciding how you would set out the area. Here are some of the things you might want to include.

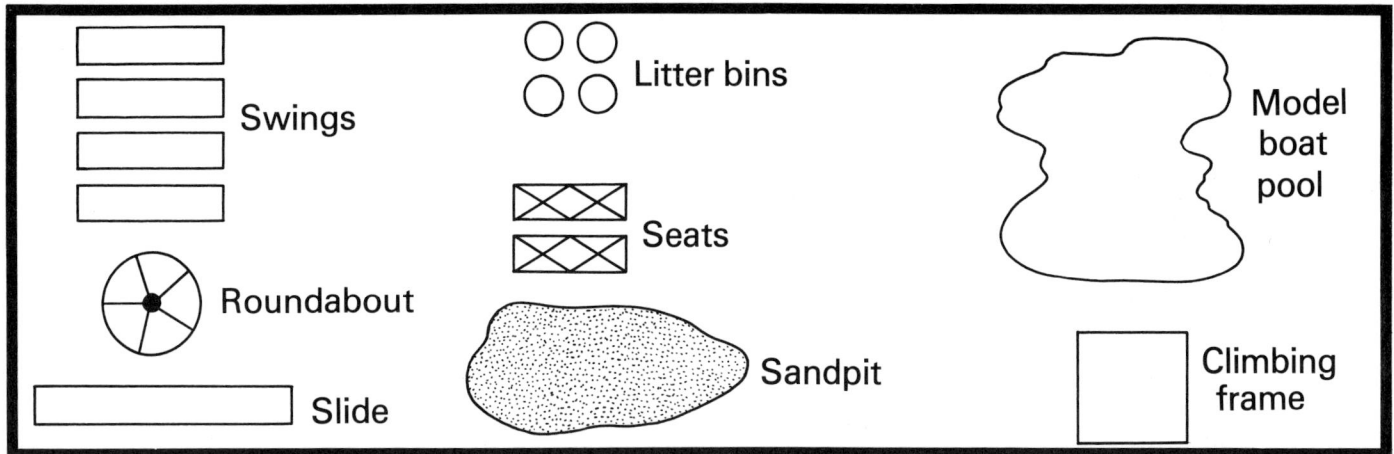

Swings

Litter bins

Seats

Model boat pool

Roundabout

Sandpit

Slide

Climbing frame

You may decide to add different items—or more of particular ones—that is up to you. When you are deciding where to locate things remember that the ground by the stream may be damp, and that the path will be important for people getting into the playground. Now make your plan, giving reasons for your decisions.

Other woods

Large woods, or forests as they are called, are not just used as playgrounds. They often provide people with jobs. The timber obtained from these forests earns valuable income for the country in which they are found.

This photograph was taken in Norway where there are large forests of cone-bearing trees (**coniferous** trees). These plantations cover many square kilometres. When the timber has grown large, and it may take 60 to 100 years to do so, it is cut down. The men who do this are called lumberjacks. The tree trunks are stripped of branches and twigs and then carried to the nearest saw mill. The easiest way to do this is to float the logs down the river. The logs are kept moving to prevent a log jam.

Eventually these logs may be made into such things as matches, but most probably into paper. By selling the paper the Norwegian people earn much money.

Describe the scene shown on the photo.
Find Norway in your atlas.
Its neighbouring country to the east also produces a lot of timber. What is it called?

Using your school or public library find out about forestry, lumbering and paper making.

The new shop

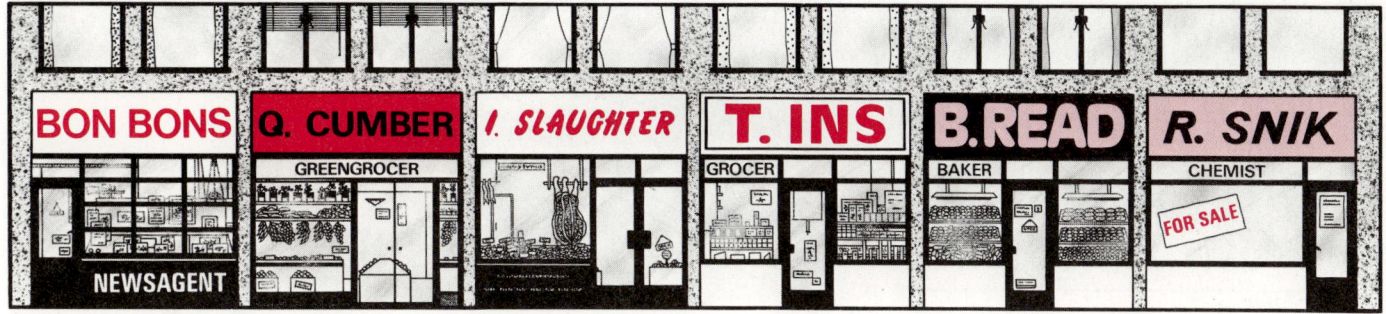

One of the shops on Parklands Shopping Parade is empty.
These people are looking for an empty shop:

Decide for which of these people the empty shop is most suitable. Do this by asking yourself these questions:

What will each of them sell?
How much space will they need?
Is there any competition?
Are there enough people nearby to make the shop a success?

Now read on:
It is not often that you find two bread shops on one small shopping parade because they would have to share the limited number of regular customers from the nearby houses.

As no one buys from a furniture store very often they need to be in places which many people can reach easily. Furniture shops also need a lot of display space.

Although we visit supermarkets quite often, they too need to be where many people can reach them. They also need lots of space. So the empty shop above seems to be most suitable as a fish and chip shop.
Were you right?

Shops, then, fall into groups:

Shops we use often	Shops we use now and again	Supermarkets and chain stores — shops we may use often but are only found where the area served by the shopping parade is very large.	"Shops" that do not sell anything but serve us in some way.
grocer newsagent	shoe shop furniture shop	Woolworth's Littlewoods	banks dry cleaners

Set out a page in your book like this and add to the lists.
Into which groups do the shops near you fall?

Local shopping

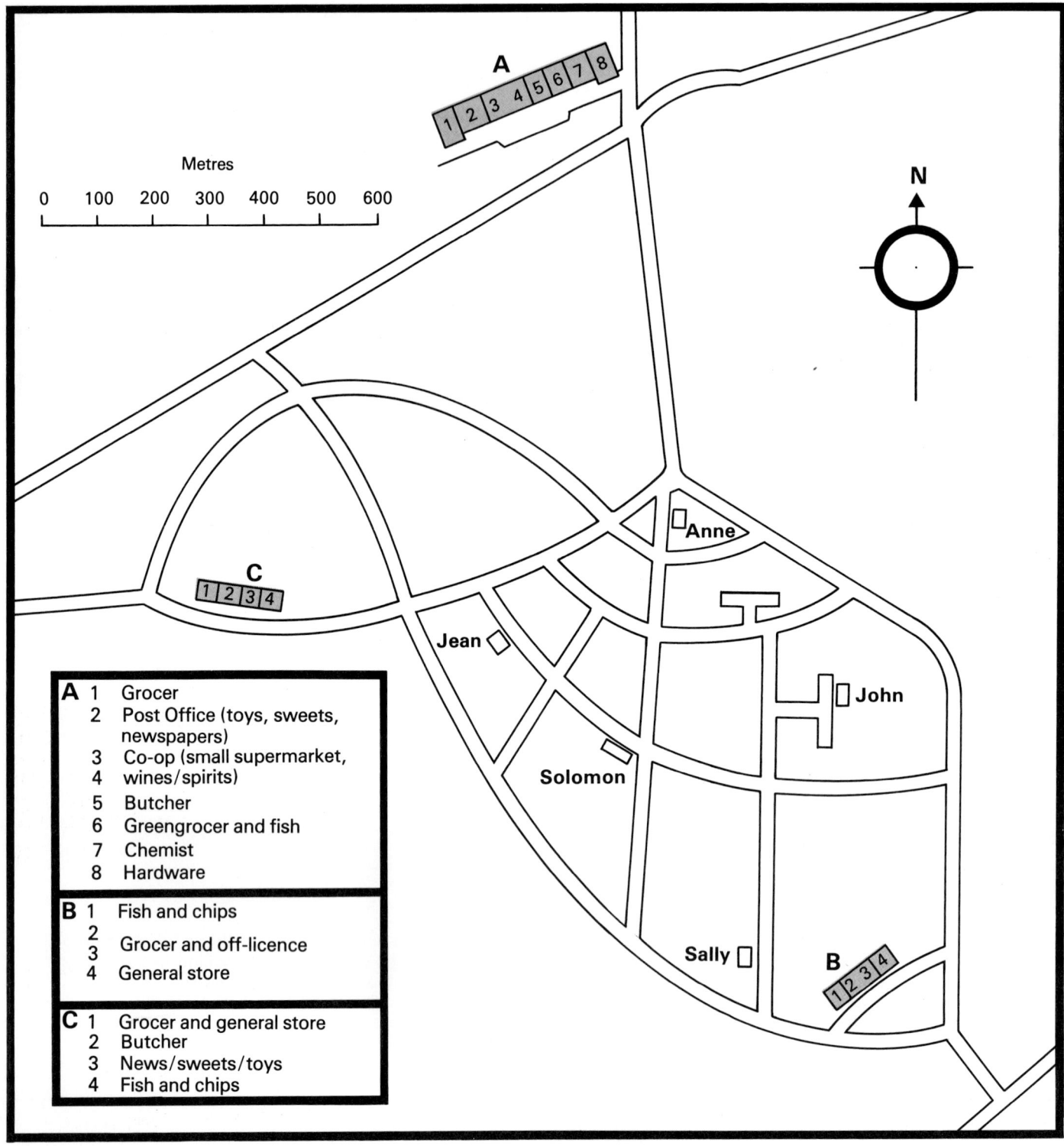

A
1. Grocer
2. Post Office (toys, sweets, newspapers)
3. Co-op (small supermarket, wines/spirits)
4.
5. Butcher
6. Greengrocer and fish
7. Chemist
8. Hardware

B
1. Fish and chips
2.
3. Grocer and off-licence
4. General store

C
1. Grocer and general store
2. Butcher
3. News/sweets/toys
4. Fish and chips

This map shows the position of three shopping parades and the homes of five people. The shops found in each of the parades are listed.

Measure the distance between the parades.
A–C = ——metres; B–C = ——metres.
Why do we have lots of small parades like this?

Which shops are found on all three parades? Are these the type of shops we visit often? Which two shops are found on only one of the parades? Do we visit these shops often?

If there is a choice most people go to the nearest shop which sells what they wish to buy.

If each of the five people on the map wanted to buy fish and chips,
  who would go to parade B?
  who would go to parade C?
  who might go to either B or C?
If the distance is the same to two shops, what do you take into account before deciding which to go to?.

On a tracing of the map:
  mark the route taken by each person going for fish and chips;
  draw lines around those parts of the map from which people are likely to use parades A, B and C.

What is the greatest distance anyone has to go to buy butter?

Whose fish and chips will be the coldest by the time they get home?
How far does Jean have to go to the nearest shops? In which direction does she go?

How far does John have to go to the nearest shops? Describe his journey by filling in the distances and directions in the following sentences:

  "When John goes to the shops he walks for

  (distance)
  ....   metres in a   ....

  direction. Then he turns   (direction)
                            ....   and

  walks for   (distance)
            ....   metres before

  turning   (direction)
          ....   and walking

  (distance)
  ....   to the shops."

Sometimes the nearest shops do not have the things we need and then we have to go further afield.

For what items would everyone on this estate have to go to parade A?
List six things they could not buy on any of the three parades shown here.
Where might they go to buy these items?

Here are some shopping lists. Decide which parade (or parades) each person will go to and draw their route on your map tracing.

Anne needs:

Cabbage
Chops
Tin of Soup
Chocolate

John needs:

Mince
Sweets
Jelly
Newspaper

Solomon needs:

Shampoo
Tin Opener
Cauliflower
Bread

This photograph shows shopping parade A.

Using the list on page 32 identify each of the shops.

At which end is the hardware store? Where is the butcher's shop? If you had only the picture to look at, what might help you to find the post office? Where will some of the shopkeepers live? Give two ways in which the flats at either end of the parade are different from those in the middle. Why do you think a shelter was built along the front of the shops?

Here is a plan of the front of the shops.

Trace it and then shade (in different colours):
the areas covered by grass
the car parking area
the parts for people to walk on
Name:
two shortcuts across the grass
two steps
the covered walk-way
the postbox

Would you like to shop here? Is it attractive? Is it safe for young children?

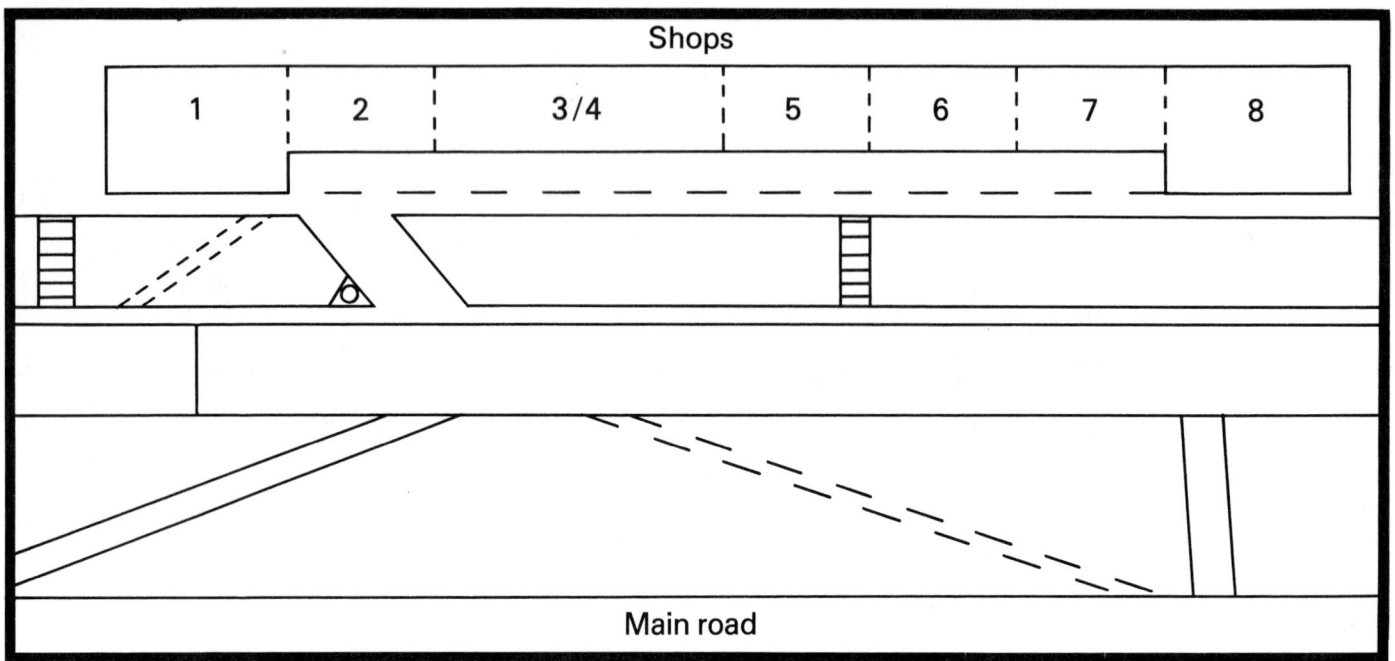

Here are pictures of the other two shopping parades that appear on the map on page 32. *Study them carefully and decide which is B and which is C. Give a reason.*

Like many buildings in this country, these have steeply sloping roofs.

Do you know why this is so?
What building materials have been used:
   for the walls?
   for the roofs?
   for the doors and windows?

At first sight the two parades look alike, but there are differences.

Give three ways in which they are similar.
Give three ways in which they are different.
What two services does the parade in the first photograph provide that the second parade does not?
How do the people living above the shops get into their homes?
Why have high walls been built between the shops?

Copy this drawing into your book and colour:
   the parts of these buildings used as shops
   (in blue)
   the parts of these buildings used as homes
   (in orange)
   the parts of these buildings used for storage
   (in red)
To give you a clue, why do you think the windows X and Y have been blocked up?

Describe one of these pictures, choosing words from this list to help you: sunny, dull; attractive, unattractive; clean, dirty; interesting, uninteresting; tidy, untidy.

The suburban shopping centre

As you discovered on page 33, we cannot buy all we need at the local shops round the corner. For some items we need to go into town or, perhaps, to a large new shopping centre like the one shown here. You may know one like it.
How different is it to the shopping parades on page 35?

How would you like to shop here? Write all the ways in which it has been made pleasant for the shoppers.
In what ways are the shops different from the shops on parades A, B and C?
Would you say it was a busy shopping centre?
Are there any signs of vandalism or untidiness?
Can you think why this might be so?

One of the pleasant aspects of shopping in a centre like this one is that there are no cars whizzing by. Shoppers have been separated from cars and lorries. The cars are at the back in a large car park—here it is.

Such shopping centres have grown up because many people have cars these days and we no longer need to walk every time we go shopping. It is important that shopping centres provide large car parks.

Find out how many square metres a parked car needs. Count up the number of cars parked in the two views of this car park. How much space do they occupy altogether?

You can see from these views that the building is not just given over to shops. Shops only occupy the ground floor.

How many floors are there above the shops? What do you think the upper floors may be used for? Do you think that the shopkeepers will live "over the shop" as in parades A, B and C? How is the shape of this building different from the other shopping parades that you have studied?

This **birds-eye** view shows another large suburban shopping centre. It is on a main road and is about four miles from the centre of a large town. The whole ground floor is given over to shops. People from the nearby houses may shop here every day but there are also many other people who shop here once a week or once a fortnight. These people arrive by bus or car.

How has the car parking problem been solved here?
Why are large centres like this one on or near main roads?
Can you estimate the length of the building? (the size of a car may help)
Why are the shops set back a little?
How have they tried to make the front of this building attractive?
How many floors has the tall block? What will it be used for? If each floor is three metres high, what is the total height of the tall block?

This shopping centre has the following shops:

shoes	1
clothes	2
electrical/hardware	2
vegetables/fruit	1
food supermarkets	2
wallpaper/paints	2
meat	1
confectionery	2
soft furnishings/carpets	1
TV rental	1
cleaners	1
Post Office	1
bank	1
books	1
Woolworths	1
empty shops	2

Group these shops under the headings:
  Shops we use often
  Shops we use now and again
  Supermarkets and chain stores
  "Shops" that do not sell anything but serve us in some way (eg banks)

Draw a graph to illustrate this

I THOUGHT THERE MIGHT BE A 'WOOLIES' IN A CENTRE OF THIS SIZE.

Wonder how Noodle knew this?

37

Where our food comes from

Here is Mrs Pickwick's shopping basket. Julie is interested to know where the different foods come from.

> I am going to mark all these places on a world map!

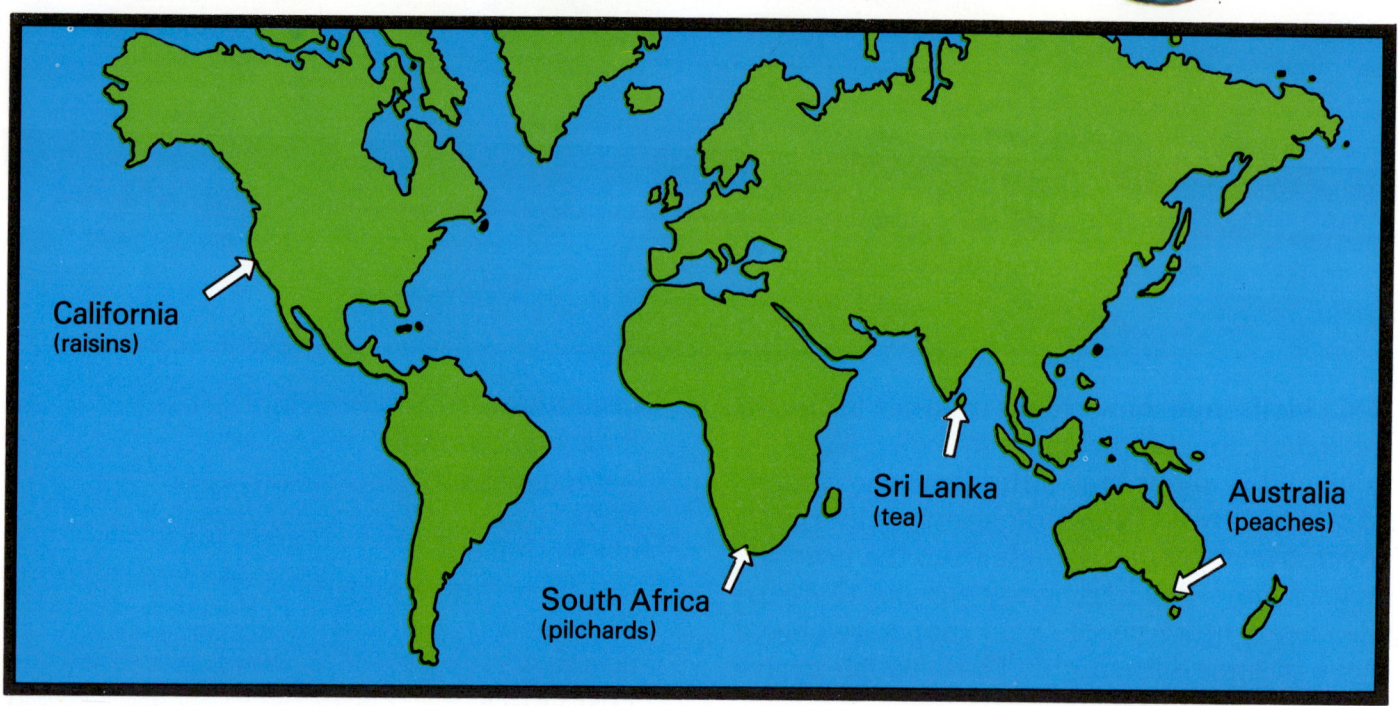

California (raisins)

Sri Lanka (tea)

Australia (peaches)

South Africa (pilchards)

Julie has started her map.

Trace the map into your book and finish it off for her.
Add to the map by looking at labels on tins and packets in your own pantry.
If you visit a fruit stall in the market ask where all the different fruits come from.
Add these to your map too.

> Don't we depend on a lot of people in other parts of the world for our food! And I'm amazed at how far some of the food has travelled.

Make a list of the foods we grow ourselves in Great Britain.

> BUT DON'T TEAR THE LABELS OFF OR YOU MAY GET BAKED BEANS FOR SWEET INSTEAD OF RICE PUDDING!

Finding out about farms

Last night I met Mr Herdman, the man who owns Mill Farm. He is a very interesting man to talk to and he asked if we would like to look round his farm one day next week.

Before we go we had better visit the library and find out something about farms — then we'll know what to look for and what questions to ask Mr Herdman.

Ooh yes Dad, we'd love to see the animals and find out how they grow things.

Here are some of the things they found out about farms:

● Farms vary in size from a hectare or two to hundreds and even thousands of hectares.

● Farms are usually divided into a number of fields.

● Farmers may keep animals or grow crops; sometimes they do both.

● Farmers have to decide in which fields to put the different crops or animals.

● In some parts of the world most of the people are farmers, in other parts very few of the people are farmers.

● Farmers are always busy but the jobs they have to do change throughout the year.

● The soil is very important to the farmer—he must keep it fertile.

● There are many different kinds of farms in the world and even in this country.

● Some farmers sell almost everything they grow, others sell very little.

● The weather from day to day is very important to the farmer.

● Some farmers own their land, others pay rent for it.

Using this information, make a list of questions that the Pickwicks might ask when they visit the farm. If you look carefully on this page you may find the answer to one of your questions.

Make a list of the crops and animals they are likely to see on Mr Herdman's farm.

I HAVE ANOTHER ONE: FARMS ARE SMELLY AND MUDDY PLACES

Do you think Noodle is right?

Turn to the map on page 12 and describe the route the Pickwicks will take to get to the farm. You could do this by drawing a simple map of your own.

At Mill Farm

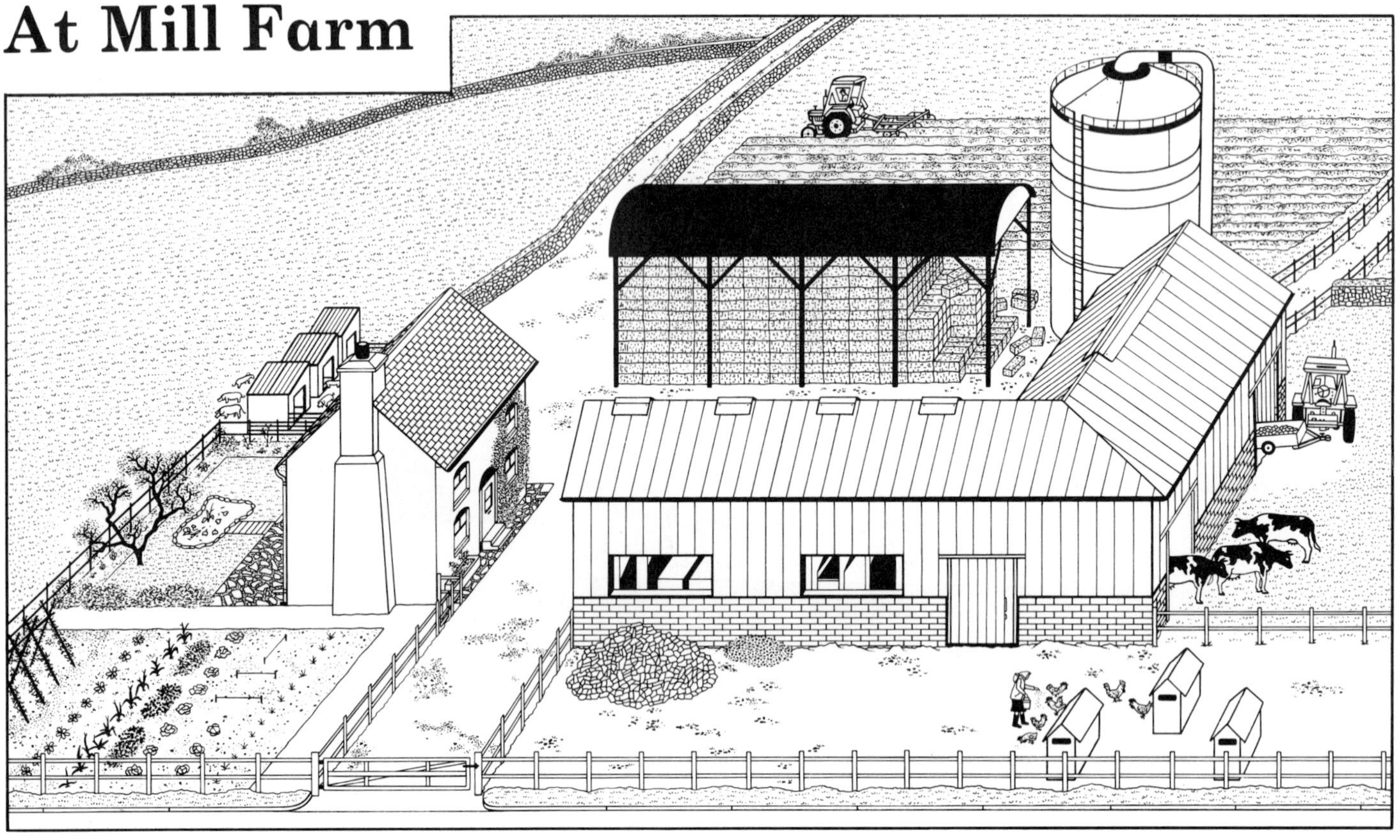

This is a view of the farm buildings.

How many buildings are there?
In which of the buildings do the Herdmans live? How can you tell?
Identify the cowshed. This is also called a milking parlour or byre.
What is the building attached to the cowshed used for?
The large building at the back is a barn. Describe the building and what it is used for.

Other buildings that you might see on a farm are stables, garages and sheds.
Find out what these buildings are used for. Can you think of a good reason why the vegetable garden is close to the house? After all, the farmer has plenty of land.

Other important features of farms are the hedges (or walls, or fences) and the gates. These are barriers, either to keep things in or to keep things out.

What do they keep in? What might happen if these got out?
What do they keep out? What might happen if these got in?

List the animals in the picture and for each, say why the farmer keeps them.
Can you see any crops in the fields?

What is Mr Herdman doing? What is Mrs Herdman doing?

Mr Herdman's day starts at 5.00am when he gets up to milk the cows.

Does he have far to go to do this job?

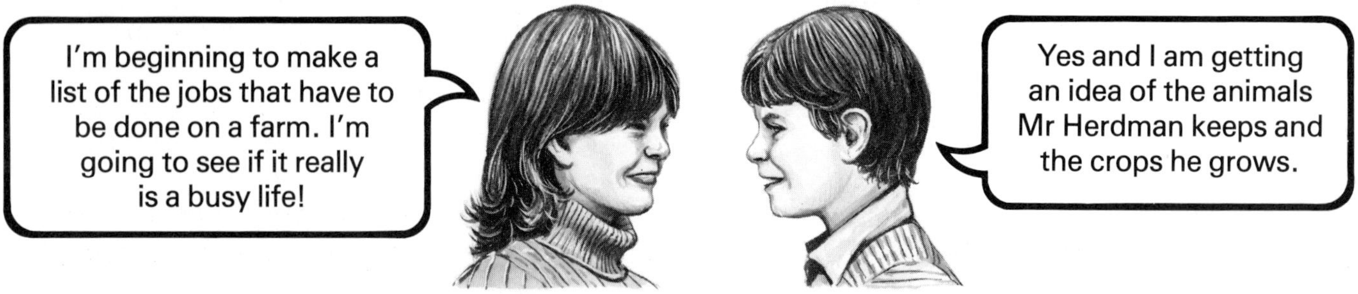

I'm beginning to make a list of the jobs that have to be done on a farm. I'm going to see if it really is a busy life!

Yes and I am getting an idea of the animals Mr Herdman keeps and the crops he grows.

Around the farm buildings

Below is a plan of the farm buildings. Copy it and label: the house; barn; milking parlour; hen houses; machinery shed; vegetable garden.

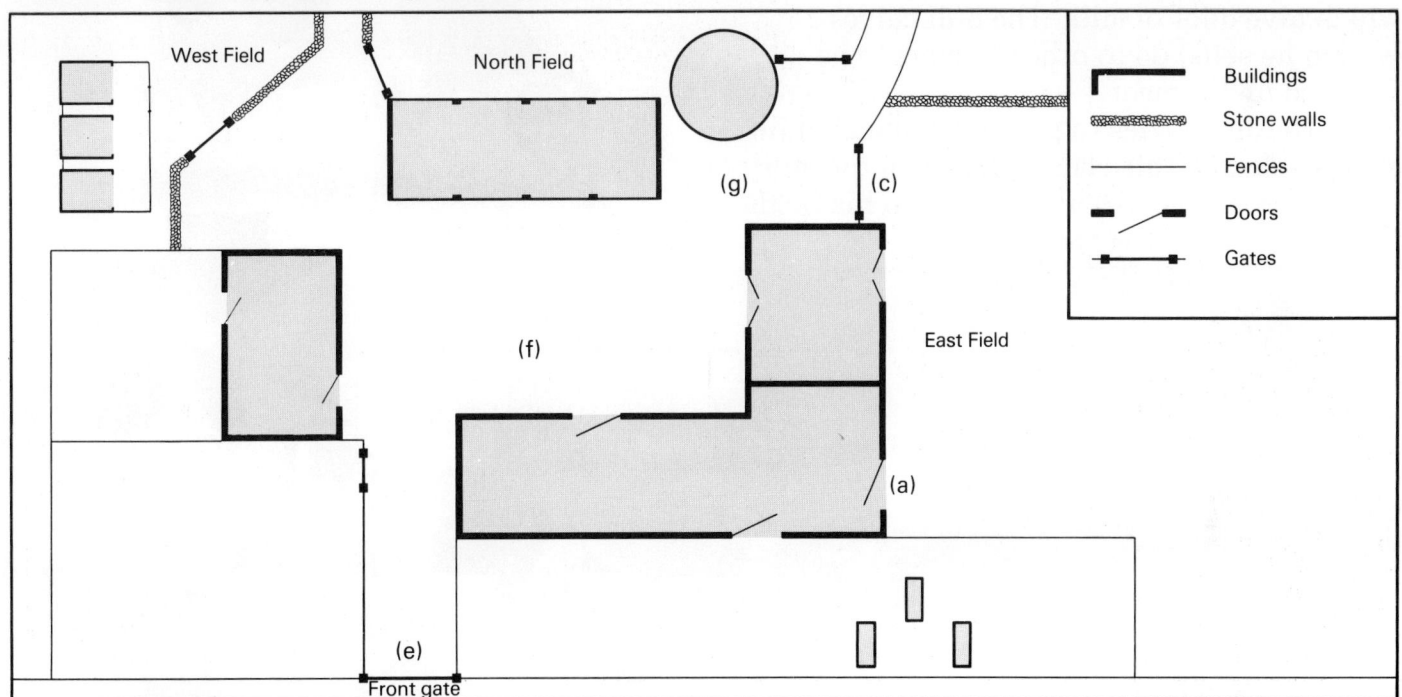

My book says farmers are always busy — can you tell me what you've done so far today, Mr Herdman?

This is how Mr Herdman's day began.

5.00am Got out of bed.

5.15am Walked to the front gate to shut it—some careless person had left it open!

5.20am Walked into East Field via gate (c) to call in the cows. They come in through door (a).

5.30am Started milking.

6.45am Finished milking. Took the cows out into East Field and walked back through the milking parlour to the house for my breakfast.

7.00am Breakfast.

7.30am Back to the milking parlour—to clean it out.

8.00am Walked into West Field to see if the pigs had enough food.

8.15am Walked into North Field to see if the ground was dry enough for ploughing. It was so I went round to the machinery shed for the tractor.

9.00am Started ploughing and I've been at it ever since.

Gosh, and it is only 11 am now!

Plot Mr Herdman's journeys on your map.
Which doors or gates did he use most?
Which building did he not go into?
Which piece of ground (e, f or g) did Mr Herdman use most?
Mr Herdman is thinking of putting up a new storage shed. *Where would you put it? Give your reasons.*
Can you list some of the things Mrs Herdman would have been doing during the morning?

41

Milk—from field to doorstep

There are a number of different breeds of dairy cattle. Mr Herdman keeps Friesians, which give a lot of milk. The bull calves (which he sells) go to other farmers to be fattened-up for meat.

Mr Herdman tries to produce as much milk as possible and this chart shows you the story of milk production from the grass in his fields to its delivery to the doorstep.

Friesian cow

Milk being collected at farm.

Cow being milked mechanically. Milk flows through pipes into tank.

Milk being tested.

Milk in large tanks - being pasteurised

Bottling plant

Milkman delivering

Using the pictures to help you, write a short account called "The story of milk".

Explain why:
    everything must be kept very clean;
    the milk has to be treated (pasteurised)—find out about a man called Pasteur;
    the milk is bottled.

Find pictures of these other breeds of dairy cattle—Jersey; Guernsey; Ayrshire; Dairy Shorthorn.

How would you recognise the different types? Where do you think the first three get their names from?

Look carefully at the diagram and map below. Write out the following sentences, choosing the correct phrase from the brackets.

A lot of farms
One farm ⎱ produce the milk which then goes to ⎰ a lot of dairies
Several farms ⎰   ⎱ one dairy
  several dairies

When the milk has been treated and bottled it goes to ⎰ a lot of houses
one house
several houses

The milk is carried to the dairy by ⎰ a lorry
a milk float   but it is taken to the houses by ⎰ a lorry
a milk float

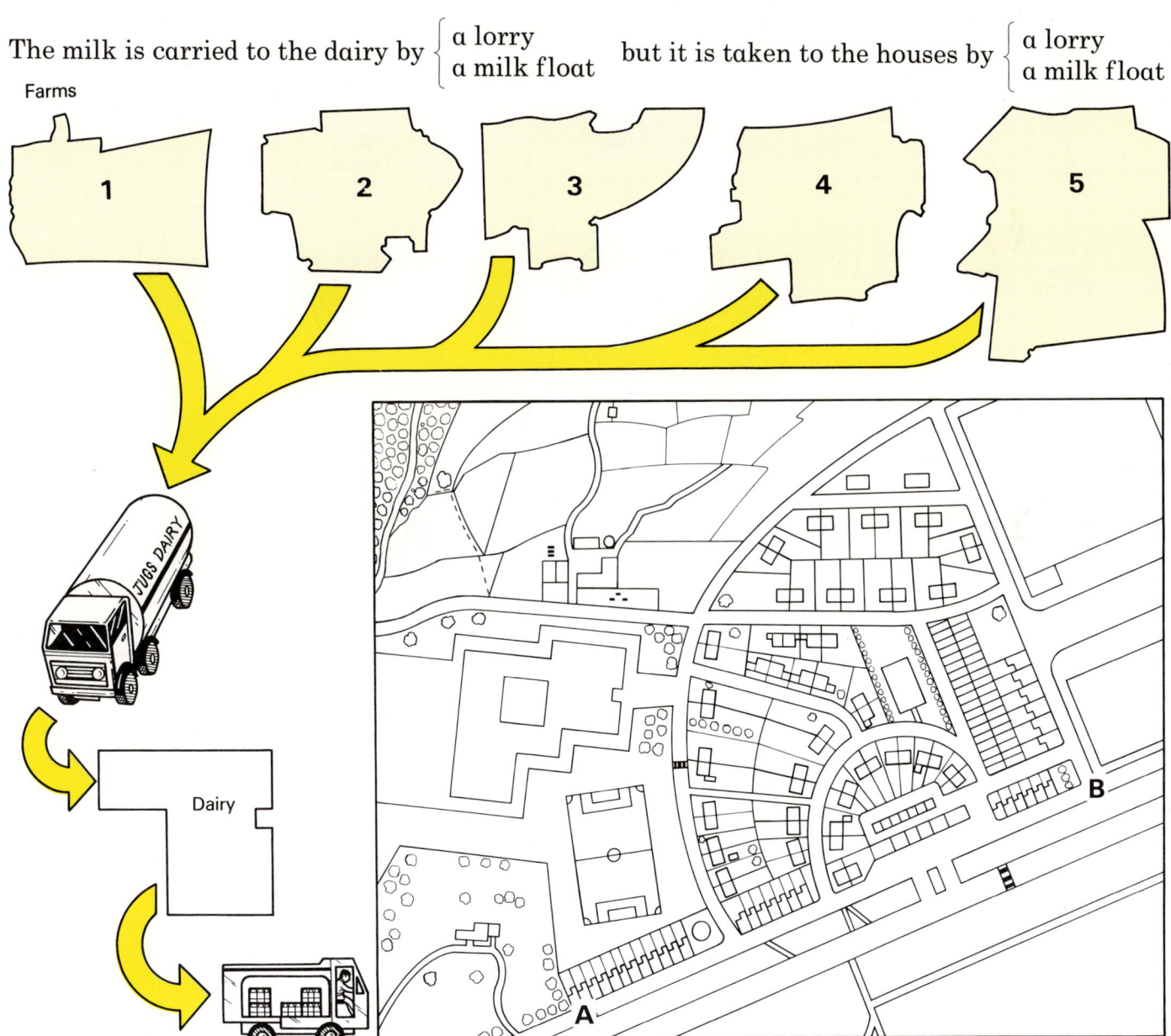

Farms

1   2   3   4   5

JUGS DAIRY

Dairy

How is your milk delivered to you? How often is it delivered?
Ask your milkman how many houses he visits on his round. From how many dairies does he get his milk?

Can you plan a good route for the milkman around the estate above, starting at point A and finishing at point B?

A map of Mill Farm

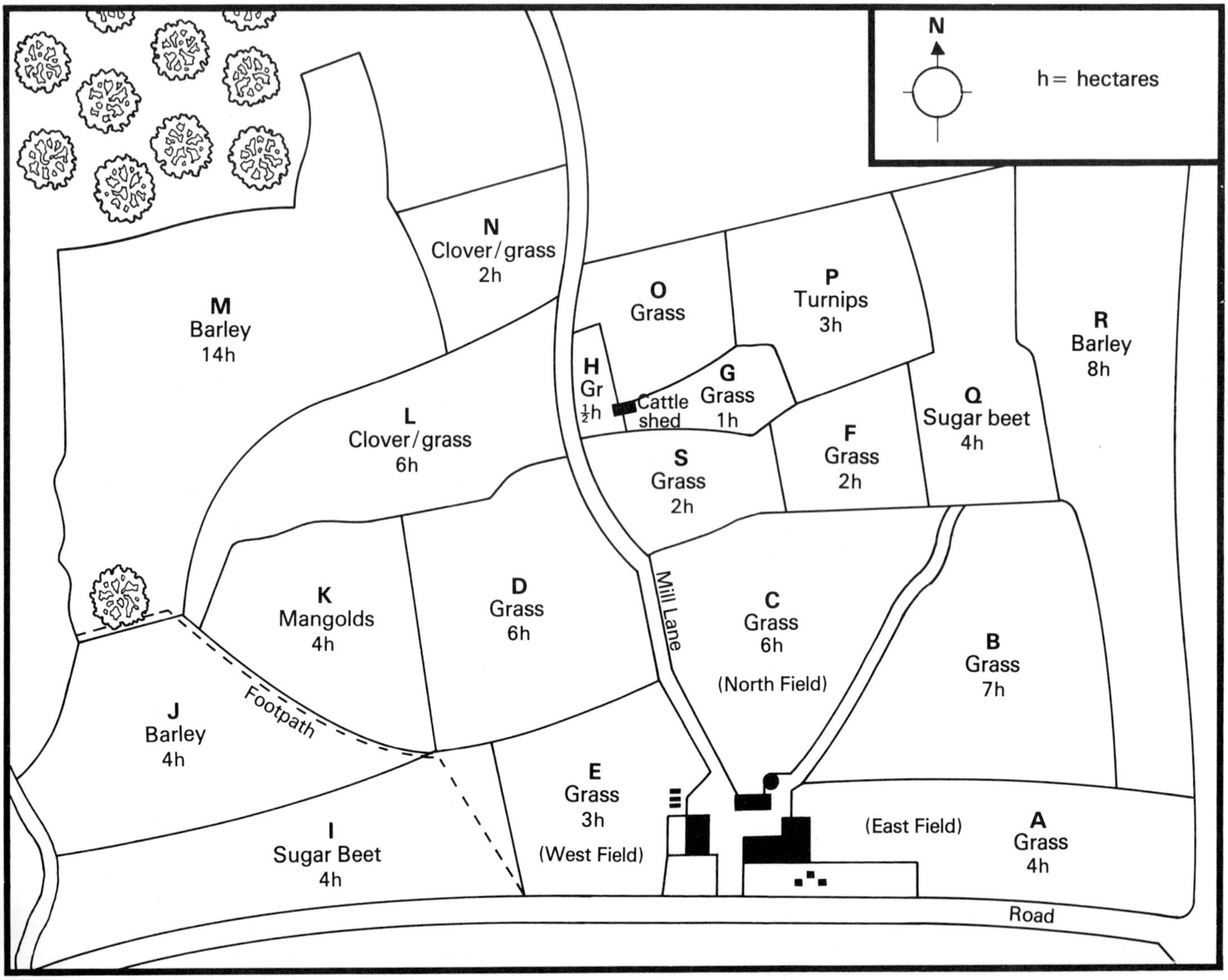

N

h = hectares

N
Clover/grass
2h

M
Barley
14h

O
Grass

P
Turnips
3h

R
Barley
8h

H
Gr
½h

Cattle
shed

G
Grass
1h

Q
Sugar beet
4h

L
Clover/grass
6h

S
Grass
2h

F
Grass
2h

K
Mangolds
4h

D
Grass
6h

C
Grass
6h

(North Field)

B
Grass
7h

Mill Lane

Footpath

J
Barley
4h

E
Grass
3h

(West Field)

(East Field)

A
Grass
4h

I
Sugar Beet
4h

Road

Here is a map of the whole farm. Notice that the farm buildings are near the road.

From what you have already found out about Mill Farm can you suggest a good reason why the farm buildings are clustered together?
Is it a good thing for the farm buildings to be close to the road?
Where should Mrs Herdman put up a sign saying that she has eggs for sale?
How many fields has Mill farm?
Which field is the largest; the smallest; the longest?
Which fields are shaped like a triangle; a rectangle; a square?
How many hectares of land are there altogether?

*How many fields grow **grass** or **clover**? How many hectares do these fields add up to? Is this about one-quarter; a half; or three-quarters of the farm?*
How many hectares of barley does Mr Herdman grow?
*How many hectares of **roots** (turnips, mangolds and sugar beet) does he grow?*
Find out why root crops are so called.

COR! THAT'S A BIG SUM

In the fields

Scene: The farmyard at Mill Farm

Mr Herdman Well, you've had a look at the map of the farm, would you like to have a look around now?

Julie Ooh! yes and you can tell us about the crops in the fields. How do you decide what to grow in each field?

Mr Herdman *(As they walk along Mill Lane)* Well, although it looks very confusing there is a pattern. When the cows are not in the milking parlour . . .

Richard You mean in the winter time?

Mr Herdman Yes, Richard—it's too cold for them to stay out from November to April. For the rest of the year they spend most of their time in fields A, B, C, D, E and, now and again, F and S. You will see on the map that these fields are nearest to the farm buildings. Because cows have to be milked twice a day, we like to keep them close by.

Julie Otherwise you and the cows would spend all your time walking backwards and forwards to the fields!

Richard Does that mean that you don't have to visit a field of barley very often?

Mr Herdman That's right Richard—once the fields have been ploughed, harrowed and sown we just have an occasional visit to put on fertiliser or weedkiller and then it's back later for the harvest.

Julie *(looking into field H)* What about these fields?

Mr Herdman I use these small fields for the calves. Once they've left their mothers they can look after themselves as long as they have somewhere to shelter in bad weather.

Richard They use the cattle shed for that do they?

Mr Herdman Yes, and when they are bigger I sell some of them.

Richard *(looking into field L and across to field M)* What about this field then and the barley field over there?

Mr Herdman Well as you know, I'm mainly a dairy farmer so most of the crops grown on the farm are fed to the cows. The clover and grass are cut and dried for winter feed—together with some of the grass from the other fields; dried grass is called hay.

Julie So that's what we saw in the barn, is it?

Mr Herdman Yes Julie. A lot of the barley and all the turnips and mangolds go to the cows too. I sell the sugar beet to the sugar factory but the tops also make good cattle food. If I have a very good crop, I'm able to sell some barley.

Richard So you sell milk, sugar beet and sometimes some barley.

Julie And calves.

Richard I was just wondering if the size of the field mattered very much.

Mr Herdman It can do—for instance I wouldn't dream of growing barley in the very small fields because I need to use a lot of machinery. For arable crops big fields are better.

Julie And what about the soil?

Mr Herdman Well the soil has to be kept fertile even if the field is growing grass.

Richard Do you grow the same crop in the same field every year?

Mr Herdman Some of the fields of grass are the same every year but the other fields have a different crop each year. It's called crop rotation and it helps to keep the soil fertile.

Julie I don't understand what you mean by crop rotation.

Mr Herdman Well, let's walk back to see the cows and I'll explain later. *(They turn back and walk towards the farm buildings.)*

Act out this scene with two of your friends.
Perhaps you could continue it?
In which direction were they walking as they went along Mill Lane?
In which direction did they have to turn to look at:
  the cattle shed?
  field L?

Find out all you can about these jobs on the farm: ploughing; harrowing; sowing; harvesting.
What is meant by **arable** *farming?*
(a dictionary or encyclopaedia will help)
Does Mr Herdman grow very much that he can eat himself?

Crop rotation

Julie is right—rotation *does* mean turning or moving around and that is just what happens in crop rotation—the crops are moved from field to field around the farm from year to year. Below you see fields I; J; K; L; M and N on Mill Farm and the crops grown in years 1979; 1980; 1981 and 1982.

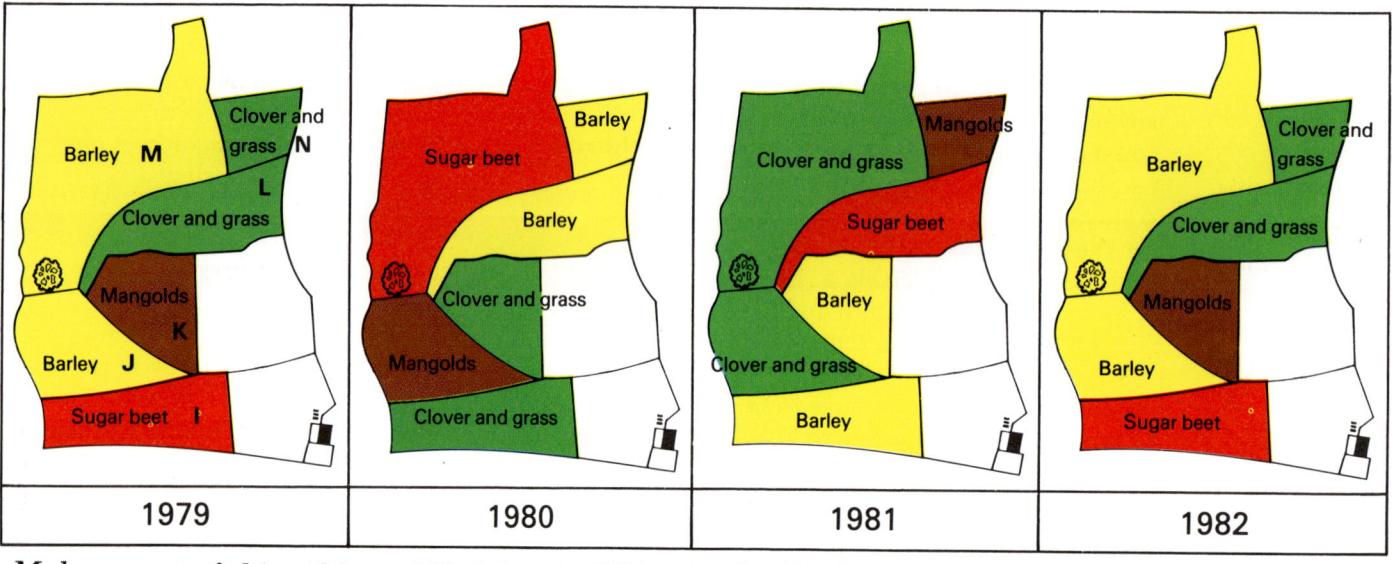

| 1979 | 1980 | 1981 | 1982 |

Make a copy of this table and finish it by filling in the blank spaces:

Year	Field I	Field M	Field L
1979			
1980			
1981			
1982			

I buy lots of bags of fertiliser to spread on the land and we also save all the manure from the cows and spread it on the land in winter — perhaps that's why Noodle thinks farms are smelly places!

Mr Herdman does not grow the same crop in the same field each year because different crops take different **minerals** (foods) from the soil. **Cereals** (barley, wheat and oats) take a lot of goodness from the soil and allow weeds to grow so he follows the barley with a root crop (mangolds, sugar beet, turnips) which keep down the weeds. The roots provide the animals with food. After the root crop he sows clover and grass which help to put goodness back into the soil when they are ploughed into the soil at the end of the third year. Barley follows this and so this simple rotation starts again.

So crop rotation is one of the ways you keep your soil fertile — what are the other ways, Mr Herdman?

The farmer's year

Mr Herdman begins his farming year in late March, when he sows his barley. In April he plants the turnips and sugar beet. These have to be thinned out by hand hoeing in late May or early June. In late June and early July he cuts grass for hay, bales it and later stores it in the big barn. The barley harvest keeps him busy in late August and during September. October is the time for ploughing. Also in October, he digs up his sugar beet and after cutting off the tops (for the cattle), he stores them until they are collected by a lorry. He digs his turnips in November and begins feeding them to the cows which have now been taken inside for the winter. In December and January manure is carted from the farmstead to the fields and spread on the land. During the winter months Mr Herdman also attends to fences and hedges and generally does odd jobs around the farm. In March he harrows the land to make a good seed bed for the barley and roots—and so the year starts again. Of course, day in and day out, he has the cows to milk twice a day.

Draw an illustrated calendar of the activities on Mill Farm throughout the year.

In and out of the farm
You have now found out enough about Mill Farm to be able to draw an input/output diagram for the farm. Such a diagram shows all the things that come on to the farm and all the things that are sold by the farm.

Draw this diagram in your book and fill in the boxes.

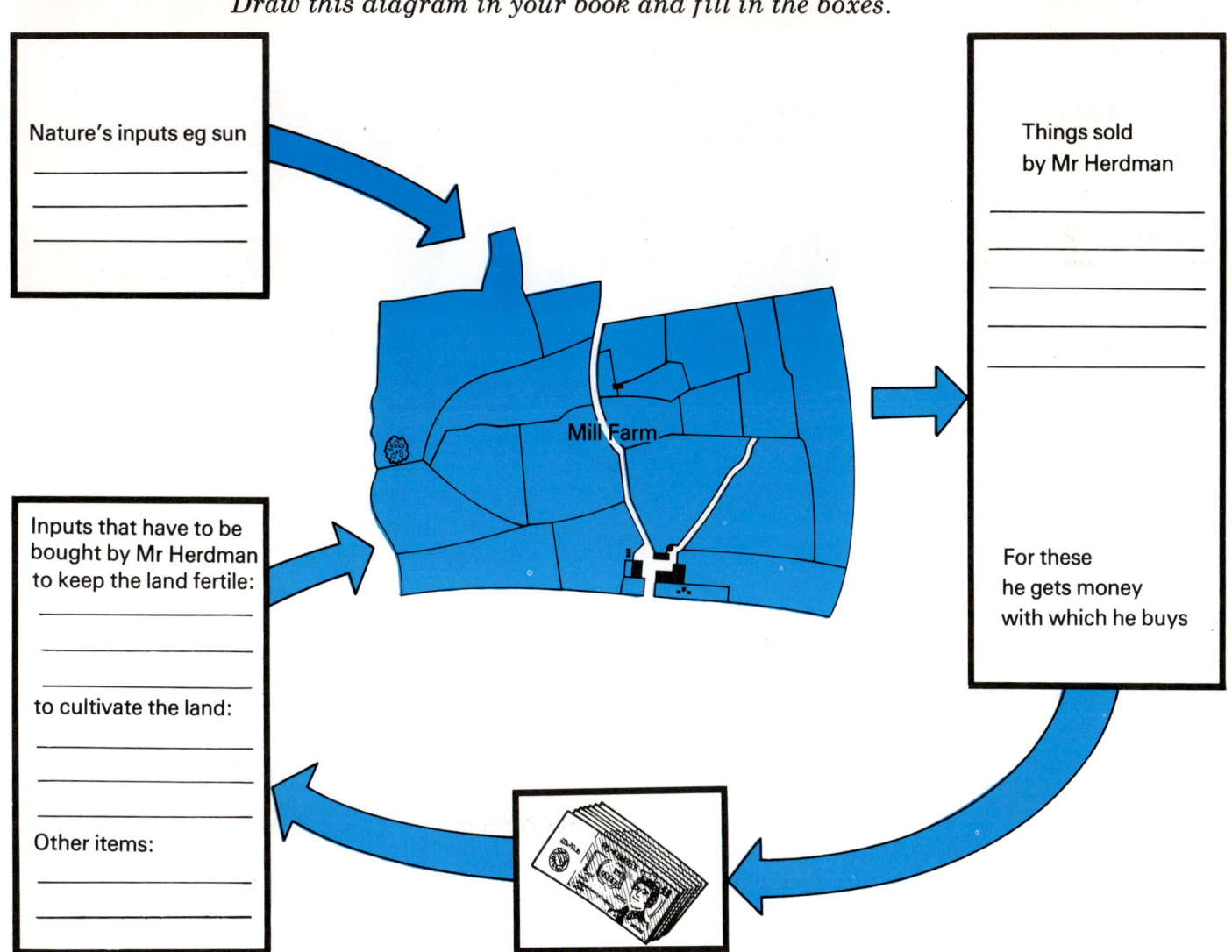

Nature's inputs eg sun
_____
_____
_____

Things sold
by Mr Herdman
_____
_____
_____
_____

For these
he gets money
with which he buys

Inputs that have to be
bought by Mr Herdman
to keep the land fertile:
_____
_____
_____

to cultivate the land:
_____
_____
_____

Other items:
_____
_____

Mill Farm

At the Roesti farm in Switzerland

Mr Herdman tells the Pickwicks that he is giving a talk in the church hall the following evening about a farm he visited in Switzerland, and suggests they might find it interesting.
They decide to go along.

'I have been asked to talk about my visit to a farm in Switzerland last year. While I am talking I will show you some photos I took while I was there.'

'This large overhang keeps the snow away from the doors and windows. They told me that they sometimes have several feet of snow.'

'This is the farm I visited. It belongs to the Roesti family and they live in a village called Kandersteg in the mountains of Switzerland.'

'The people were very friendly and showed me round. The children knew a lot about the place as they help out when they get home from school.'

'You can see that most of the building is made of wood.'

'This is where they keep their equipment.'

'This is where the animals used to be kept. Swiss mountain farmers used to keep their cows in the same building that they themselves lived in. Then they didn't have to go out to the cow shed in winter when there was a lot of snow about.'

'This is the water trough.'

'Here you can see where the family live. They keep their house very neat and tidy.'

It's amazing how much information you can get from one picture. I can see one way the Roesti family travel about. Can you? I can also see what is growing on the mountain side. Can you?

You could draw a picture of the Roesti farm and label it. Find out where Switzerland is from your atlas. Can you find out about farms in any other countries? How are they different?

"Mr Roesti is a dairy farmer, like me. The farm did appear to be quite prosperous but Mr Roesti told me that he had had some help from the government. A few years ago he built a large new barn and cow shed behind his old farm. He only uses the old farm house for living in and for storing equipment now. Beside his farm is a plot of land where he grows vegetables but otherwise all his fields are of grass. It is all that he can grow in the short growing season that will provide enough food (or fodder) for his cows.

This is the new barn and cow shed. As you can see most of this building is also wood, though not all of it.

Can you see the pile of manure stacked outside on the right? This was later spread over the fields as a fertiliser. Roesti says it is cheaper and better than using chemicals.

Can you see the pile of wood? The family use wood for burning in their fire and cooker, so they need to have plenty. Can you suggest where it has come from?

You can see the smart new tractor, too.

This photograph shows the village of Kandersteg. Roesti's farm is in the distance on the right. You can see the way the farms are scattered over the floor of this valley. This is because land suitable for farming is scarce. The bigger buildings are hotels and some of them are very fine.

Can you see the river in the bottom of the valley? The steep rocky sides of the valley? The forests? The railway?

Many of these trees have been planted to stop avalanches. Can you find out what an avalanche is? The railway goes through a long tunnel in the mountains. The Swiss people seem to be very good engineers.

This shows another part of the Roesti's farm. It is up on the mountain side; what the Roestis call their alp. In summer when all the snow has gone Roesti takes his cows up the mountains so that they can graze on the mountain grass. While they are there one of his family looks after them. He or she lives in a small hut on the mountain side during the summer. Other members of the family stay in the valley and collect the hay from the fields, which they store in the barn. This hay is then fed to the cattle when they are living in the cow shed during the winter months. It also shows how steep the ground is, and how stony. The small building is used for storing hay to feed the cattle."

Describe what you would like and dislike about living on the Roestis' farm.
Which of the photographs do you find most interesting? Why?
Try to collect information and pictures about other farms in other lands. Compare them to Mr Herdman's and Mr Roesti's farms.

From farmyard to factory

Mr Herdman is a dairy farmer. He makes money by keeping cattle and selling their milk. Other farmers nearby rear pigs which they fatten up and sell to a factory in the neighbourhood. Here sausages, pork pies and other foods are made. Sandra's mum works in the sausage factory and Mr Pickwick suggested that she might be able to tell the family about her work. Later, when they asked her, Mrs Kirkpatrick spent some time showing them pictures and describing what was happening.

Every morning lorries arrive at the factory bringing pigs from 20 farms nearby. In all, about 1000 pigs are brought in each week. They are put into pens at the factory. The pigs are slaughtered, inspected and chilled. The next day they are cut up.

Jim is cutting the pigs with a mechanical saw.

Shoulders, middles, sides and legs go into the curing department. After eight days the bacon is sold to shops either whole or as pre-packed bacon slices. Some of the legs and shoulders are roasted and sold as cooked meat. In this picture Jenny is inspecting packets of bacon.

The bakery is one of the busiest departments in the factory. It produces thousands of pies and sausage rolls each day. Here is Tom getting sausage rolls ready to put in the oven.

In your own words, write a short account describing how sausages are made.

Write about one of the people in the pictures. Mention the clothing they have to wear, the machinery they work on, and the building they work in.

Draw a simple flow diagram to show how pork pies are made.

Carry out a "Sausage survey" in your class by asking such questions as:

    Would you like to work in a sausage factory?

    Do you like/dislike sausages?

    What sort of sausages do you like best?

    How many sausages can you eat for dinner?

Write up the results of your survey.

FANCY! ALL THIS JUST TO GET MY BANGERS AND MASH!

All products are packed and made up into orders. Vans are sent out each night and morning to supply shops and restaurants.

A large variety of sausages (180,000 per hour) comes off the production line. There are loose-linked, slicing and skinless, as well as hamburgers.
    This machine is operated by Mavis.

Eric the lorrydriver makes 35 calls each day. He has a very early start at 5.00 am, to make sure the pies are in the shops by 9.00 am.

Another factory

The following day the Pickwick family went out for a walk. As they went along they talked about the things Mrs Kirkpatrick had told them. "You know now that a factory is a building or place where things are made", said Mr Pickwick. "Or **manufactured**!" replied Julie. "Good Julie, you've picked up a good word there," replied Mr Pickwick. Richard, not to be outdone, then said, "The things made in a factory are called **products** and products are made from different materials." "Aren't they called **raw materials**?" asked Mrs Pickwick. "Yes", said Mr Pickwick, "the raw materials arrive at the factory and then the workers make them into finished products for us to buy. Tell me, what were the raw materials going into Mrs Kirkpatrick's factory and what finished products did the factory produce?"

Can you answer Mr Pickwick's question?

After walking on for a few more minutes the family found themselves looking at this scene:

This is another kind of factory—it is a power station. The raw materials used are coal and water and the end product is electricity. This flow diagram shows what happens.

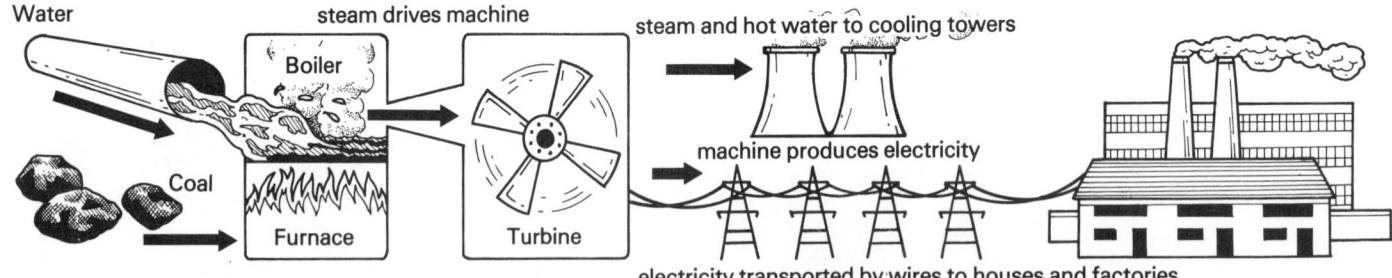

Draw similar flow diagrams to show how:
wool from the sheep's back is made into a blanket;
a log of wood is made into a door or a window frame;
iron ore dug from the ground is made into an iron girder.

Make a list of six things made from: wood; iron or steel; wood and iron.

Noodle appears to be learning! He could collect pictures of factories as well.

I'LL COLLECT PICTURES OF DIFFERENT MANUFACTURED GOODS AND ARRANGE THEM IN SETS

Trace an outline of the picture above and on your tracing name these features:
the square rectangular parts of the factory that contain the machinery
the tall narrow chimneys that take the smoke away from the boilers
the cooling towers—in which the water is cooled before being returned to the river
the railway lines
the high rise blocks of flats
the playing fields

How big is the power station compared to a house?
Describe what the factory looks like.

The industrial estate

Sometimes you see a number of factories built fairly close together. We talk of this as being an industrial area. Occasionally on the outskirts of big towns there are estates which have only factories on them. These are called **industrial estates.**

This photograph shows such an industrial estate on the outskirts of a big town.

Describe what the area looks like. How many different factories can you find? Why do you think it is important that these factories are built or located near to a main road? How many lorries can you count at the factory in the foreground?

Here is an unusual view of part of an industrial estate. It was taken from an aeroplane flying directly over the estate. *Can you see the roads? You can just see a number of cars in the car park on the left, and several lorries behind the building. Can you see any trees?*

Make a list of any factories which can be found in your area. What do they produce? Some parts of the country specialise in making different things. Can you find out which part of the country is important for making cars?

A week's weather

The weather in this country is always changing and this makes it interesting to study. By **weather** we mean the state of the air around us at any one time. Richard and his friend Tersame decided to keep a weather record. With the help of their teacher they made a chart like the one below and, at the same time each day, filled it in by answering the questions at the head of the columns. They made it more interesting by adding little drawings and symbols. This is what the chart looked like at the end of the first week.

I HAVE THREE GOOD WORDS HERE....

PRECIPITATION

TEMPERATURE

VISIBILITY

TO WHICH COLUMNS DO THEY REFER? USE A DICTIONARY IF YOU HAVE TO

	Is it: hot warm cool cold	Is it: windy breezy calm	Is it: dry raining lightly raining heavily showers snowing	Is it: clear and sunny cloudy with sunny periods overcast	Is the wind blowing from: north east south west	Can we see very far?
Monday	Cool	breezy	raining heavily	overcast dull	west	Quite a long way
Tuesday	warm	calm	damp	foggy	west	Very little
Wednesday	warm	breezy	Showers	white clouds sunny periods	west	A very long way
Thursday	cool	windy	raining heavily	overcast dark clouds	west	Not very far
Friday	cold	breezy	snow showers	overcast dark clouds	north	Not very far

54

Richard and Tersame have certainly collected a lot of information. It was not a very nice week but they have found out how changeable the weather can be.

Look at the chart carefully and answer these questions:

In which season do you think they were completing the chart? Say why.
What types of weather did they not have during the week?
Can you think of any other drawings they might have used to illustrate their chart?
On the days when it rained, where was the wind blowing from?
What kind of weather did the west wind bring? the north wind bring?

Richard and Tersame have discovered that the type of weather depends a great deal on the wind. In winter an east wind brings very cold frosty weather because it is blowing from the cold land mass of Europe. West winds, because they blow from the Atlantic Ocean, bring mild weather in winter and cool weather in summer, hence the saying:

"Wind in the west suits everyone best."

Sayings like these were attempts by people in the old days to forecast the weather. Wind direction, sky colour, and the behaviour of plants and animals helped them do this. Here are some more old fashioned "weather forecasts".

Clear moon, frost soon.

Red sky at night, shepherd's delight,
Red sky in the morning, shepherd's warning.

Swallows skimming low, bad weather on the way,
Swallows flying high, good weather on the way.

See if you can add to this list of old weather sayings.
Keep a weather record like the one opposite and see if there is any truth in such sayings.
For your weather log see if you can think of some better symbols and illustrations than Richard's.
Can you discover any more connections between wind, temperature, type of clouds, and so on?

Temperature

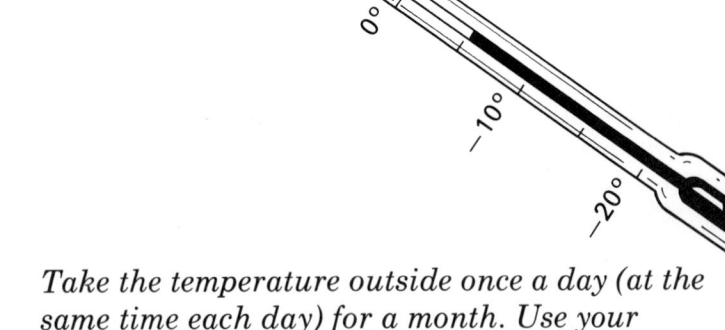

Measuring

A **thermometer** is used to measure temperature, that is, how hot or cold it is. When the liquid (mercury or alcohol) at the bottom of the thermometer becomes warmer, it expands and rises up the tube. As it cools it contracts and drops down. The numbers on the scale show the temperature.

What temperature is showing on this thermometer?
Use a thermometer to measure the temperature in different parts of your school, both inside and outside. If you have a plan of the school, plot these temperatures on it. Where are the warmest and coldest places? Can you explain the differences? Are the coldest places in windy or draughty spots? Is the warmest place near the boiler room?

Take the temperature outside once a day (at the same time each day) for a month. Use your readings to draw a temperature graph like the one below.

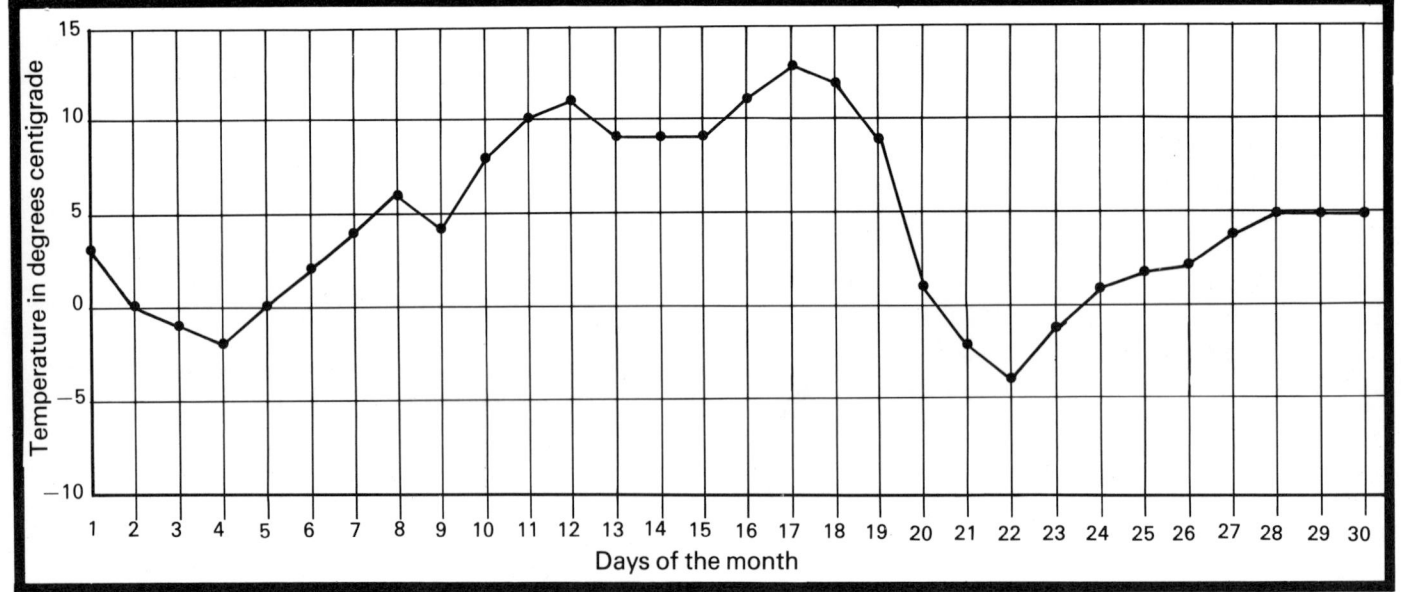

Recording

On a piece of graph paper put the days of the month across the bottom and temperatures up the side. Every day put a dot on the graph to show the temperature you have read. Join your points by straight lines and you can see whether the weather is getting warmer or colder from day to day.

In the month shown here:
    what was the highest temperature recorded?
    what was the lowest temperature recorded?

on how many days did the temperature fall below freezing point?
what temperature was recorded most often?
find the average temperature for the month by adding together all the readings and dividing the answer by the number of days in the month (30).

Ask yourself the same questions about your own graph.

We often find interesting pieces of information about the weather in the newspapers. Let's see what we can find out from these items. They all refer to the same day.

This tells us that in the last 24 hours in London the lowest (min = minimum) temperature recorded during the night was 7°C and that the highest temperature (max = maximum) recorded during the day was 18°C.

How many degrees difference were there between the maximum and minimum temperatures?
What were the maximum and minimum temperatures for Manchester on the same day?

This cutting tells us where the warmest places were in Britain on the same day.

Look up the places in an atlas. In which part of the country are these places found? North or south?

This cutting, which is part of a long list, tells us about weather conditions in other parts of the world.

Look up the places in your atlas.
Can you think of any good reasons why London, Amsterdam and Luxembourg all have low temperatures and Alexandria and Luxor have very high temperatures?

Make a collection of cuttings from newspapers about temperatures in different areas.

LONDON READINGS
Min temp (7 p.m. to 7 a.m.) 45F (7C); max temp (7 a.m. to 7 p.m.) 64F (18C); rain nil; sun 12·3 hr.

MANCHESTER READINGS
For the 24 hours to 7 p.m. yesterday: sun, 11·5 hr; rain, nil; max temp, 14C (57F); min, 6C (43F).

In Britain yesterday (daytime): warmest Brighton, Yeovilton, Southampton 66F (19C); coldest Binbrook 41F (5C); wettest Guernsey 0·12in; sunniest Littlehampton 12·9 hr.

CONDITIONS AT HOME AND ABROAD

		°C			°C
Ajaccio	f	17	Las Palmas	s	21
Alexandria	s	24	Lisbon	f	19
Algiers	f	21	Locarno	c	20
Amsterdam	c	12	London	dr	11
Athens	s	22	Luxembourg	c	12
Barcelona	c	16	Luxor	s	38

s—sunny; c—cloudy; r—rain;
sl—sleet; f—fair.

PHEW! — THE HIGHEST TEMPERATURE EVER RECORDED WAS 57.7°C IN LIBYA IN 1922 — AND THAT WAS IN THE SHADE! — THE HIGHEST TEMPERATURE RECORDED IN BRITAIN WAS 38°C AT TONBRIDGE KENT IN 1868.

RECORD RECORD

BRRRRRR! THE COLDEST PLACE TO LIVE IN IS A VILLAGE IN SIBERIA CALLED OYMYAKIN ~ THE TEMPERATURE WAS AS LOW AS -71°C IN 1964 !!! THE LOWEST TEMPERATURE EVER RECORDED IN BRITAIN WAS -27°C AT BRAEMAR SCOTLAND IN 1895 !!

Wind

We need to know two things about the wind—where it is blowing from (wind direction) and how fast it is blowing (wind speed).

For measuring direction we use a **weather-cock** or a **wind vane.** In both cases the arrow points to where the wind is coming from. This is the wind direction.

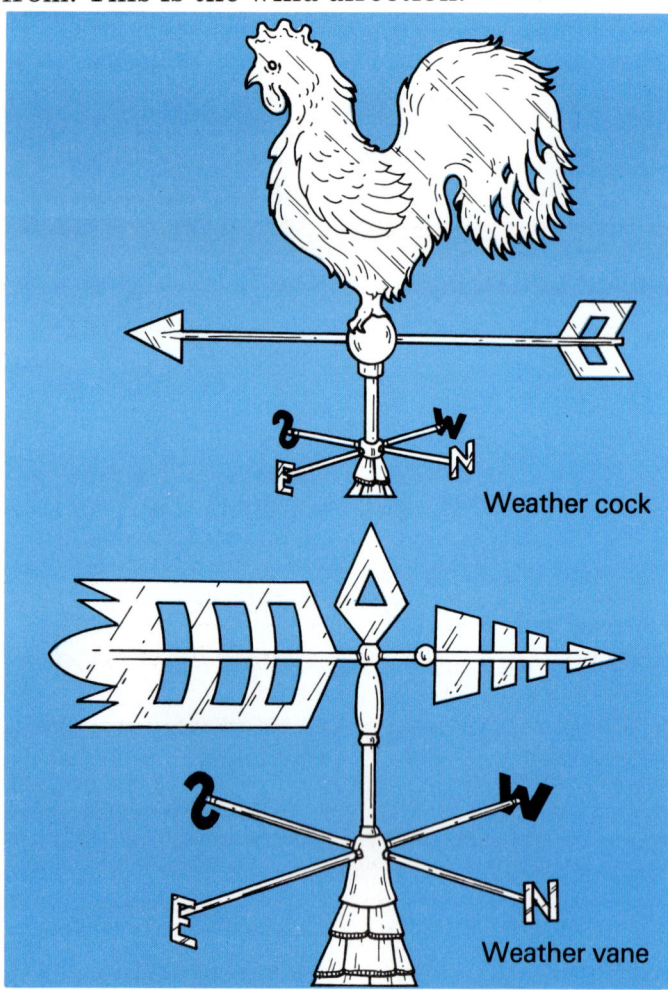

Weather cock

Weather vane

What wind directions are being shown by this weather cock and this wind vane?

As Richard and Tersame found out, the direction of the wind is important for our weather.

Find out what kind of weather we might expect to get when:
   the wind blows from the south in summer
   the wind blows from the west in summer
   the wind blows from the east in winter
   the wind blows from the north in winter.

The direction of the wind is recorded on a **wind rose.** This wind rose shows the direction of the wind for ten days—a box was shaded in for each day that the wind came from that direction.

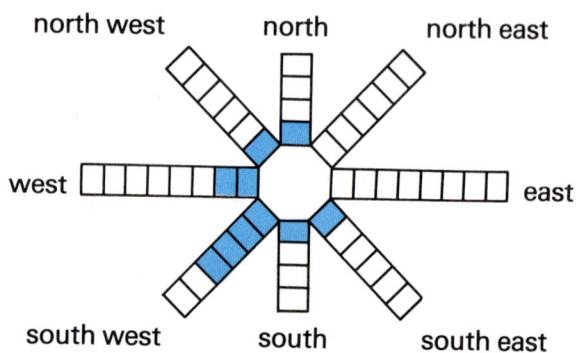

From which direction did the wind blow most often?
From which directions did no winds blow?

Make a note of the wind direction each day for a month. Record your results on a wind rose like this one. There may, of course be some days without any wind at all.

Experiment
Wind is moving air. What makes air move? This little experiment will help you understand.

On a still day fasten strips of paper to a window that is near a radiator—as in the picture. As the air near the radiator heats up it rises. Cold air sweeps in to take its place. This air in turn is heated, rises and more cold air comes in. Two "winds" have been formed, a cold one coming in to the room and a warm one going out.

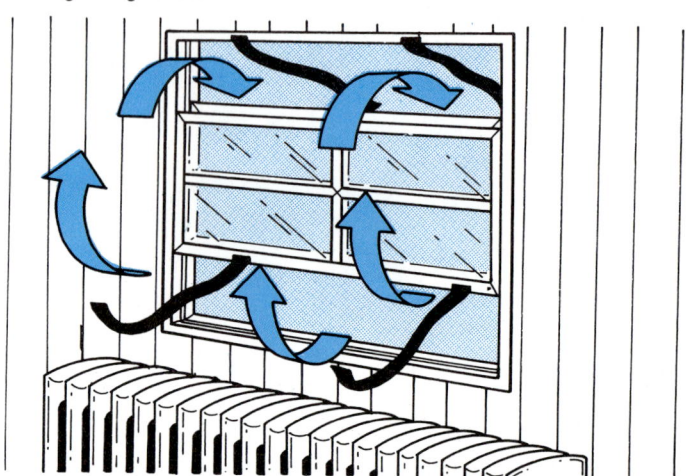

To measure wind speed we use either an **anemometer** or the **Beaufort Scale.**

The wind catches the cups and spins them around, faster or slower depending on the speed of the wind.

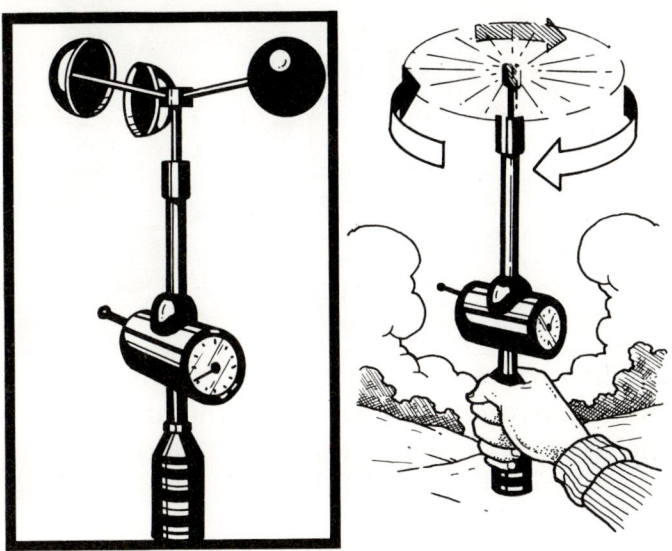

Making an anemometer like the one above is difficult but you could try making one like this:

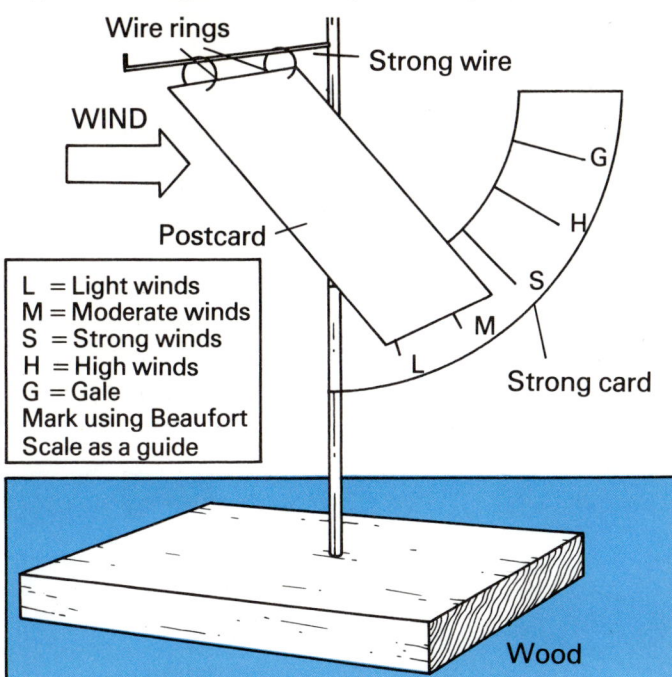

L = Light winds
M = Moderate winds
S = Strong winds
H = High winds
G = Gale
Mark using Beaufort
Scale as a guide

Use the Beaufort Scale to mark the curved scale.

Admiral Beaufort, who lived in the nineteenth century, thought of this interesting way to judge wind speeds.

	THE BEAUFORT SCALE		
	Beaufort Number	Wind	Effect over land
Light winds	0	Calm	Smoke rises vertically
	1	Light air	Smoke drifts
	2	Light breeze	Leaves rustle, wind felt on face
	3	Gentle breeze	Leaves move, light flag is extended
Moderate winds	4	Moderate breeze	Dust and loose paper blows about. Small branches move
	5	Fresh breeze	Small trees sway a little
Strong winds	6	Strong breeze	Large branches sway, wires whistle
High winds	7	Moderate gale	Whole trees sway, hard to walk against the wind
Gales	8	Fresh gale	Twigs break off trees, very hard to walk into wind
	9	Strong gale	Chimney pots and slates blown off. Large branches down
	10	Whole gale	Trees uprooted, serious damage to buildings
	11	Storm	Very rare inland, causes widespread damage
	12	Hurricane	Disastrous results

These pictures illustrate two of the wind speeds on the scale.

Can you decide which wind speed they illustrate? Draw or paint pictures to illustrate some of the others.
Using the Beaufort Scale, record wind speeds for a month.

RECORD
PECORD

HIGHEST WIND SPEED EVER RECORDED – 371 KPH ON MT. WASHINGTON, NEW HAMPSHIRE, U.S.A., 12TH APRIL 1934

Water in the air

The air around us is made up of several gases. One of these is **water vapour**—it is always there but you cannot see it. All day long, water from oceans, rivers, lakes, ponds, puddles, and plants is changed into water vapour (gas) by the sun's heat. This is called **evaporation**.

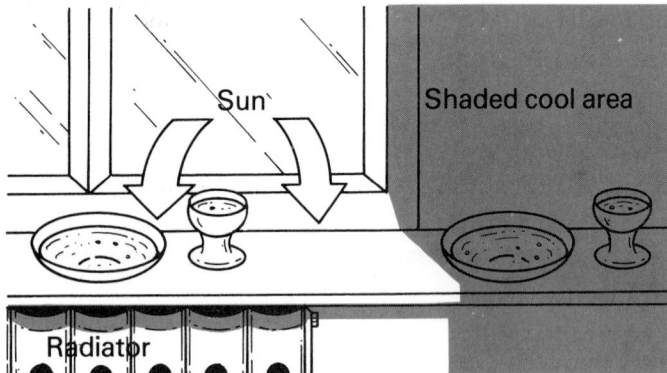

Try this experiment.

Put the same amount of water in two saucers and two egg cups.

Place one egg cup and one saucer in a warm place, and the other egg cup and saucer in a cool place.

Which evaporates most quickly? Does the water with a large surface area (in the saucer) evaporate faster or slower than the water in the egg cup?

Evaporation is speeded up by wind.

Now try this experiment.

Wet a piece of paper. Tear it in half. Lie one half down while you hold the other half in the wind (or blow on it). Which dries first?

THAT EXPERIMENT IS A WASTE OF TIME— EVERY ONE KNOWS THAT WASHING DRIES BETTER ON A WINDY DAY!

The amount of water vapour in the air varies. Warm air can hold more than cold air. The amount of water vapour in the air is called **humidity**—a kind of dampness. If air is cooled the water can change back into water or **condense**.

OH!— I ALWAYS THOUGHT THAT WATER WAS GETTING THROUGH THE GLASS

Water condensing

Water condenses from the air when it comes into contact with the cold sides of the glass.

When the air around us is cooled the water vapour in the air changes into tiny water droplets and clouds form. The clouds move with the wind and, under certain conditions, the water returns to earth as rain (or snow or sleet).

Clouds

If we want to know whether it is going to rain or not we usually look up at the sky and particularly at the clouds. Clouds are made up of millions and millions of tiny water droplets, too small to fall to the ground. However, if the droplets grow bigger they become too heavy to stay in the air, the cloud begins to look dark and it may rain.

Clouds are interesting and the experts can tell a great deal by watching them. Here are four types for you to look for:

Cirrus clouds are high in the sky and appear thin and wispy against the blue sky. They are made of ice crystals. The wind blows them into feathery strands called **mare's tails.** They usually mean that the weather is changing.

Cumulus clouds are like fluffy balls of cotton wool with flat bottoms. Shapes are always changing. They mean fair weather unless they build-up into the next type:

Nimbo-stratus are the dark, ragged, shapeless clouds of a wet day. *Stratus* means *layer* and *nimbus* means *cloud*—but usually a rain cloud.

Cumulo-nimbus are thunderclouds. They tower up to great heights and are dark at the base. When these form on a hot day they usually lead to thunder storms with heavy rain and, sometimes, hailstones.

Measuring rainfall

Rainfall is measured in a **rain gauge**—a funnel leading into a bottle. Every day the rainwater is poured into a special measuring jar.

It is not easy to make an accurate rain gauge like this because the funnel and tube are a special size, but you can collect rain in a large tin each day and compare the amount of rain from day to day.

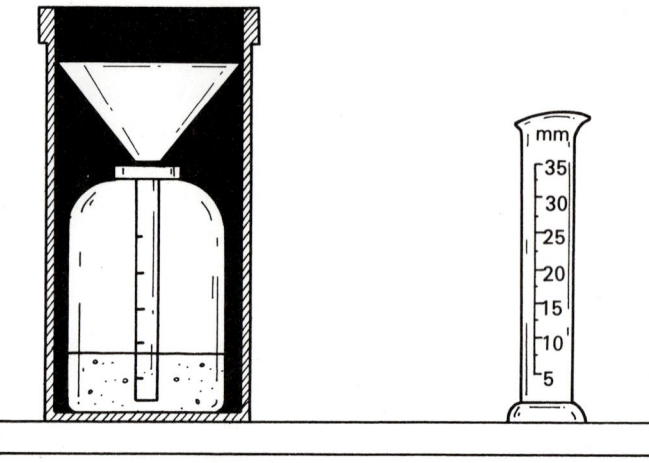

A rain gauge

For a month, rainfall is *recorded* like this: ▼

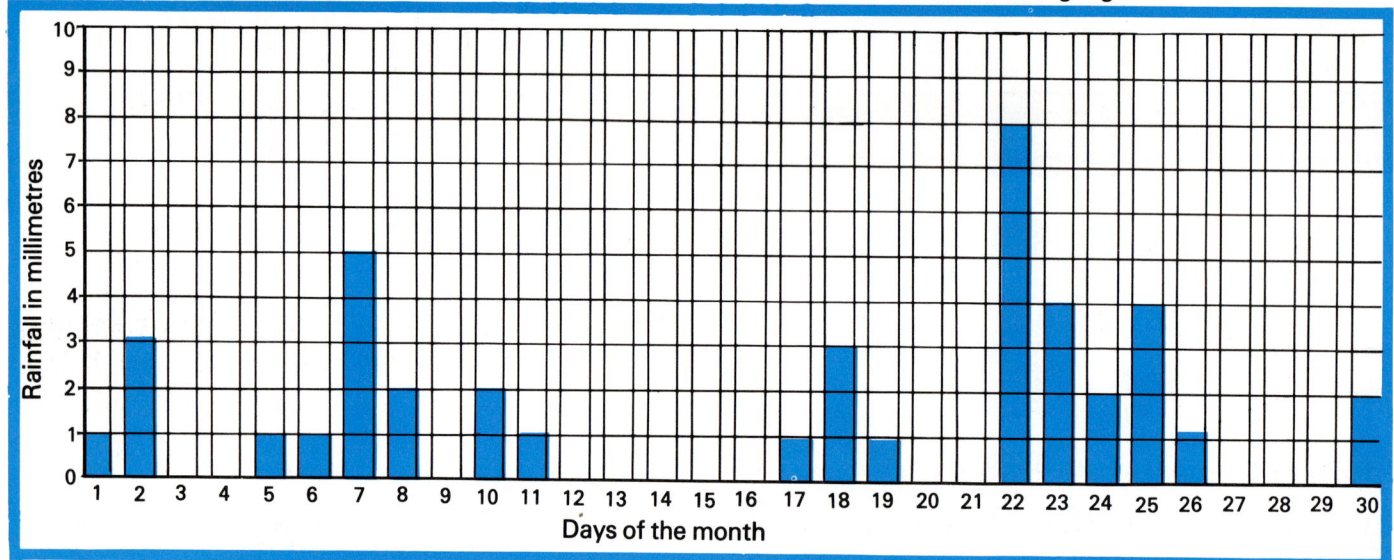

Which day had the heaviest rainfall? How much fell on this day? How many rainy days were there in this month? How many days had no rain? How much rain fell altogether in this month?

For a year, rainfall is *recorded* like this: ▶

Which month has the heaviest rainfall? Which month is the driest? What was the total rainfall for this year?

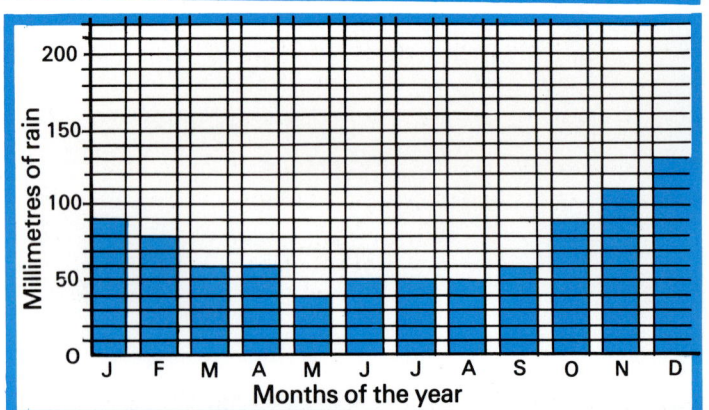

The greatest rainfall in one day was 1,870mm at Cilaos, Reunion, in the Indian Ocean on the 16th March 1952.

The highest in Britain was 279mm in one day at Martinstown in Dorset, on the 19th July 1955.

Measure 1,870mm on your classroom wall.

Air pressure

ALL THIS TALK ABOUT WEATHER IS ALL VERY WELL BUT CAN YOU PROVE TO ME THAT THERE REALLY IS AIR ALL AROUND US?

See if you can answer Noodle's question by asking yourself these questions:
Do I ever see it?
Do I ever hear it?
Do I ever feel it?
Do I ever smell it?

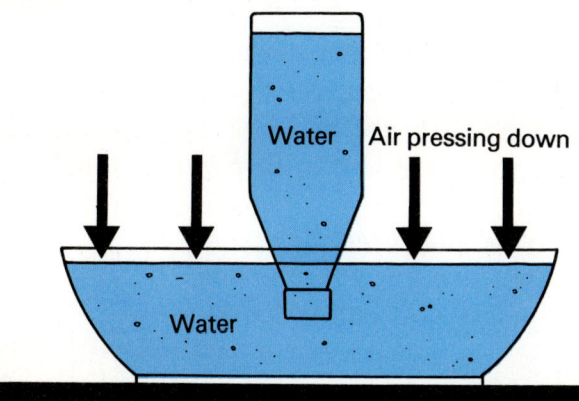

Water — Air pressing down

Water

Air also has weight. Here is an experiment to show this.

Push a bottle under water so that it fills up. Then, keeping the neck of the bottle under water, hold the bottle in an upright position. The weight of the air pressing down on the surface of the water keeps the water in the bottle. This weight is called **air pressure**.

Now do you believe that there is air all around us, Noodle?

Air pressure changes quite frequently. These slight changes are important in weather study because they cause winds to blow. Winds blow from areas where the pressure is high to areas where the pressure is low.

Air pressure is measured by a **barometer.** The first barometer was invented by a man called Torricelli in 1643. He filled a long narrow tube (open at one end, closed at the other) with mercury and stood it upright in a

bowl of mercury. The mercury stayed in the tube to a height of about 760mm. By putting a scale behind the tube we can measure changes in pressure.

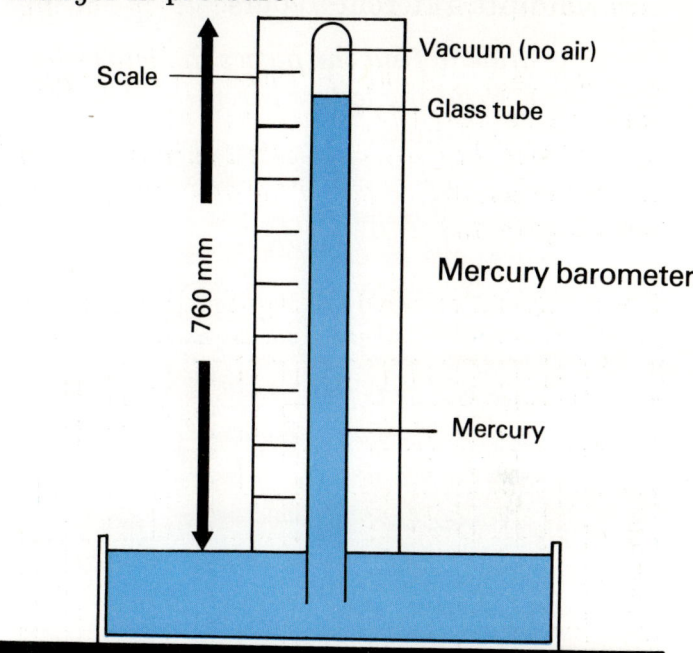

Scale

Vacuum (no air)

Glass tube

760 mm

Mercury barometer

Mercury

You may have a barometer like the one below. It works in a different way but it still tells you about changes in pair pressure and what type of weather to expect in the next day or two.

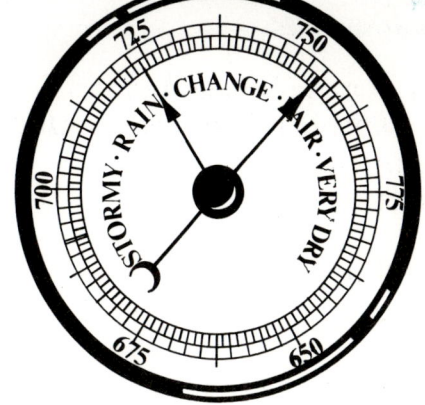

725 · 750 · STORMY · RAIN · CHANGE · FAIR · VERY DRY · 700 · 775 · 675 · 650

A household barometer

See if you can "read" this barometer by filling-in the blank spaces in these sentences:

When air pressure is very low the weather is likely to be _____ .
When air pressure is very high the weather is likely to be _____ .
If I hear Dad say "The glass (barometer) is falling," I know the weather is going to get _____ (better or worse?).

Weather in other parts of the world

Here are extracts from three letters written by people living in other parts of the world with weather quite different to ours.

Use your atlas to find the places the letters have come from. Read the letters carefully and then answer the questions.

the building. You will be interested in the weather here — everyday is the same. The sun rises at 6 am. in a cloudless sky and the heat begins to build up. A cool breeze gets up about 10 am. but dies away in the early afternoon and white cumulus clouds appear in the east. These get larger and darker. Suddenly there's a great rush of wind, flashes of lightning, crashes of thunder, and down comes the rain — in sheets. After an hour the rain stops, leaving everything dripping, battered, but a little cooler. Everyone comes to life in the evening but the next day it starts all over again. Enjoying myself but it is so hot and sticky! They do tell me that not all the days are like this with best wishes Carlos

PARA BRAZIL

Fill in this chart to describe the weather on one day in Para.

Morning	
Afternoon	
Evening	

What sort of clouds did the cumulus build up to in the afternoon to give thunder, lightning and rain? (See page 61.)

Describe how you would feel if you had to spend a month in Para.

El Kharga Egypt   27th. March
Dear Frank,
      Don't know whether I'm going to be able to stand this heat! At 6 am. the thermometer reads 37°C and this is the coolest part of the day!!! By midday it's 43°C with a hot wind. At 6.pm. the wind drops but that only makes it feel hotter still. It's impossible to sleep before 2. am, when it does cool off a little. At 5.00 am. the sun rises. I've heard it hasn't rained for 15 years and I used to grumble about the English weather. You can't imagine the

In which year did it last rain?
When did you last have rain?
What is the hottest temperature you have known?
What is the highest temperature ever recorded in Britain? (See page 57.) How much hotter was it in El Kharga?
Imagine you were sent to El Kharga to work. Describe:
  what you would feel like
  what problems you might have
  what you would enjoy/dislike most.

Tolstoy Way, Yakutsk
USSR 13th Jan.
Dear Jean,
      When I went out this morning (in my fur parka of course) the temperature was −56°C!! When it is so cold you hardly dare breath in case your lungs freeze. Your breath hangs in the air like smoke. One of our hens got out last week and was frozen solid within 10 minutes! The sky is greenish-blue and I wear sunglasses all the time because of the glare of the snow. It will be like this for another 2 or 3 months, what a mess there will be when it melts! I was

Describe the coldest day you have ever known.
What is the lowest temperature we have known in Britain? (See page 57.)
How much colder was it in Siberia when this letter was written?
Imagine you have to visit a friend living in Siberia. Write about:
  how you feel about having to go there
  what you would have to take with you
  what you would miss most about the weather at home.